Teaching Right and Wrong:
moral education in the balance

Mene, mene, tekel, upharsin
Thou art weighed in the balances, and art found wanting.
(Daniel, 5)

Teaching Right and Wrong:
moral education in the balance

Edited by Richard Smith and Paul Standish

Trentham Books

First published in 1997 by Trentham Books Limited

Trentham Books Limited
Westview House
734 London Road
Oakhill
Stoke on Trent
Staffordshire
England ST4 5NP

British Cataloguing in Publication Data
A catalogue record for this book is available from the British Library
ISBN: 1 85856 084 5

Designed and typeset by Trentham Print Design Ltd., Chester
and printed in Great Britain by The Cromwell Press Ltd, Wiltshire.

Contents

Introduction

This book is a response to renewed and widespread public interest in moral education. In the UK this interest has been given a particular impetus by the publications of the School Curriculum and Assessment Authority (SCAA) on this topic and on spiritual education. Those publications in their turn were in part responses first to the 1988 Education Act's intention of placing education in a context which includes the spiritual, moral and cultural development of pupils and of society, and second, and paradoxically perhaps, to the reduced emphasis on moral education that has been argued by some to be an effect of the National Curriculum.

But our concern is not just with documents that may soon come to seem ephemeral. The occasion for the renewed interest in moral education has a broader background, one that can hardly have been missed by anyone who keeps up with our daily news. The appalling murders of two year-old Jamie Bolger and of headteacher Philip Lawrence stand out as nightmarish aberrations and yet as somehow symptomatic of a more general moral destitution in our society. It is neither sensational nor merely politically opportunistic to see them in this way. For there is a widely-shared conviction that things have somehow gone badly wrong. These concerns are shared beyond the boundaries of the UK. Throughout the Western world, in Eastern Europe, in South Africa, in China, the kinds of problems that moral education raises have become matters of acute concern, matters to which politicians are increasingly required to respond.

Probably every age is inclined to look with dismay at its own younger generation and to lament a supposed fall in moral standards. With the millennium nearly on us concern threatens to rise to an almost superstitious *fin de siècle* anxiety. A variety of factors – unemployment, recession, the decline of the church, family breakdown, sex and violence on TV, the stuff of the tabloids, of video nasties, and of 'adult' satellite channels – seems to have coalesced to produce a malaise that leaves many people at a loss. Cultural pluralism, many believe, causes confusion. We are writing in the wake of a general election and following a period of eighteen years of Conservative government. But these problems are not simply to be laid at the door of those in power, however much incidental damage they may have done to the moral as well as the social fabric of society. We are dealing with issues that lie at the heart of modern life and it would be naive to look to politicians for easy solutions. Neither are the problems simply to be blamed on teachers themselves, with their alleged weakness for the heresy of progressivism, nor on parents – as well lay the blame on 'people'.

Writing about moral education has its dangers, particularly that of seeming to suggest that moral education, like the dental brace, is only for the young, their elders being automatically so educated and straightened in virtue of seniority (or perhaps just crooked beyond redemption). Literature on moral education often conveys a curious sense of looking on from the sidelines, as if values were only problematic in terms of how they are to be got across to children and teenagers. We hope we have avoided this tendency here, and certainly many of the contributors below emphasise how all of us, of all ages, move constantly in a world of moral shadows and moral complexity. We hope too that we shall not seem to have concurred too readily in the assumption of moral decline. The case for saying that young people in general are *more* morally aware than previous generations is surely at least as good as the case for saying that they are in some sense morally worse. In their sensitivity to (for example) issues of gender and race, in caring for the environment and being prepared to fight to safeguard it, and in their concern for social justice, the moral standing of young people at the end of the twentieth century seems to bear comparison with that of any other generation.

Of course there is mugging, there is hooliganism, there is joy-riding and the spread of graffiti. (If these misdemeanours are characteristic of the young, then mention should be made of the older generation's specialisms, such as tax-evasion, road-rage, adultery.) But as aspects of our social world deteriorate for a complex variety of economic and other reasons, and a social underclass is ever more firmly established, it is tempting to speculate that the young have to an extent fallen victim to the desire for scapegoats. In recent years to be badly off has been somehow already to be blameworthy, and evidence that poverty and social deprivation are directly related to health, regardless of diet and exercise, has been ignored or suppressed. To be a young, single mother has invited the charge of 'fecklessness', to the neglect of explanations which foreground the function of motherhood in bring meaning and a sense of purpose to an otherwise bleak and hopeless life.

These are examples of the strange turn that renewed insistence on the importance of morality has taken in recent years. A proper insistence on the irreducibility of personal responsibility, not to be shuffled off on the grounds that 'it's all society's fault', has begun to lead to a denial of the part played by social and political factors: a refusal to accept, for example, that unemployment is causally linked to crime and despair. It is as if responsibility has been privatised along with so much else; or as if, where genuine political discussion on all kinds of issues has become muted by the steady convergence of the main political parties, it is morality instead that becomes the focus for posturing debate and the setting up of straw opponents as the targets for partisan disagreement.

Given this context, it is unsurprising that discussion of morality becomes heavily polarised, with Absolutism and Relativism appearing like rival football clubs, the exclusive candidates for supporters' loyalty. The media do no service by presenting 'moral debate' in terms of these stereotypes. At one end of the stadium, runs the fantasy, there are Absolutists cheering for iron rules, principles and commandments: thou shalt do this and avoid that, or get a good kicking. At the other end Relativists are supposed to be found declaring that everything is a matter of opinion, you mustn't impose your views on others, and It All Depends – a standpoint more properly described as subjectivism, as noted below. From this end of the stadium perhaps we hear the strains of *You'll Always Walk Alone*.

Although this crude caricature, like most caricatures, contains grains of truth thorough-going absolutists and relativists are actually thin on the ground. Nevertheless the polarisation is dangerous: it lends itself to the creation of bugaboos. From one point of view, absolutism is cast as a spectre to dismiss the place of principles in the moral life and, worse, to suggest that we might be better off without talk of morality altogether. (*Ought* we to stop talking of morality, we might reply? *Ought* we to avoid making value judgements? These 'oughts' themselves have moral force.) From the other point of view, fear of the dragon of relativism deters us from acknowledging the complexity and diversity of the moral life, the fact that so much *does* depend on the particular circumstances, even if 'it all depends' must be the start of moral thinking rather than its conclusion. The effect of these bugaboos is to prevent us from exploring and trying to find our directions in what might be called the middle ground of morality, the shifting and uncertain terrain in which we live the great part of our moral lives.

It is this middle ground that our contributors attempt to map. What is presented here is not a coherent and unified theory of moral education, or even a theory at all. In general we are inclined to be suspicious of systematic theory and the kinds of ways it might come into moral education. (For similar reasons, and in line with ordinary usage, we have avoided systematic differentiation between 'morality' and 'ethics' in this book.) Often we think that it is *bad* theory that has led to the prevailing approach, especially where morality is understood in narrow terms with the result that its deep and pervasive importance in our lives is obscured; often there is an artificiality about the language of moral education as if once it enters the classroom or the seminar room, or, let it be said, the political debate, it dresses up for show. Thus the reader will not find in these pages detailed analysis of recent academic literature on moral education with careful rebuttals and counter-arguments. In general, we think that that literature doesn't get things right. There is something missing in current discussions of moral education that is not merely of peripheral importance. It is not a particular set of topics that have been overlooked or a particular persuasion that is under-represented. Rather it is the whole picture of morality that needs to be changed.

The concern of this book, then, is to deepen discussion. Those who come to it expecting to learn directly 'how to do moral education' will be disappointed. Those who take the view that morality, like anything else that needs to be learned, can adequately be dealt with in a discrete subject on the curriculum may find what we have to say obscure and puzzling. Why do we not take the opportunity to help schools and parents by showing how moral education should be delivered? We take the view that morality is not like this and that to think of it as an ingredient that might be missing and could be added is already to have got the whole picture wrong.

Our contributors are writing in a climate where to discuss moral education in any but the crudest terms is to invite hostility and misrepresentation.

SCAA too has a problem in that the proposals made in its short pamphlets are further reduced to the soundbites of the media, making them all the more vulnerable to criticism. In expanding on the SCAA proposals Marianne Talbot and Nicholas Tate have provided an excellent starting point which gives a sharp focus to our discussions. We are doubly grateful to them: first, for the clarity and appropriateness of their chapter, and, second, for their willingness to contribute to a project which they knew would in many respects be critical of their work. Most helpfully they have also provided a section from SCAA documentation which is presented as a coda to their chapter. In the concluding chapter we try to address directly the kinds of issues that are presented by Talbot and Tate. We choose not to introduce the rest of our chapters but rather let them set their own scenes, each in its distinctive voice.

We are dealing with matters that in one sense are timeless but in another strangely topical and uppermost in the minds of teachers, parents, governors, and politicians concerned with education. It was imperative to us to find a publisher who would be able to get our ideas into print quickly so that we could contribute to that discussion. We are delighted then to express our thanks to Gillian Klein and to Trentham Books for providing exactly the service that we needed and for providing this with efficiency, tolerance and good humour, and style. Thanks are also due to the Universities of Dundee and Durham for support with this project.

Chapter I

Shared Values in a Pluralist Society?

Marianne Talbot and Nick Tate

'If we are supposed to instil values in the young, then *whose* values are we supposed to instil?' This question is asked, usually rhetorically, at every meeting on moral education that we attend or address. It has struck at the heart of schools' confidence in the teaching of values. But the force of this question is deceptive. The question has a simple and empirically justifiable answer: namely, '*our* values, the values to which *every* person of goodwill would subscribe'.

It was partly because of the deceptive force of this question, and the way in which it has been undermining the confidence of schools and teachers, that SCAA set up the National Forum for Values in Education and the Community. In this short paper we intend to outline the background to the setting up of the Forum, the remit given, the Forum's findings and the results of our consultation on them. We will also discuss, in some detail, some of the objections that have been brought against part of the Forum's findings, showing that each of these objections misses its mark. The Forum's other findings will not be discussed in detail.

The Forum was set up on the recommendation of delegates to SCAA's conference *Education for Adult Life*. This conference, held in January 1996, was organised in response to the concern, expressed by many teachers, heads, governors and parents, that so much time and energy had been spent on the promotion of pupils' academic development that their spiritual, moral, social and cultural development was being neglected. SCAA was being left in no doubt that many people believed the consequences of this to be potentially disastrous. Which of us, after all, wants their child to leave school clutching a handful of certificates, but with no idea of how to be a human being? That the conference coincided with the tragic death, at the hands of a 16 year-old, of the headteacher Philip Lawrence, was a stark underlining of this concern.

Delegates to the conference agreed that a Forum should be set up and given a two-fold remit, as follows:

- to discover whether there are any values upon which there is agreement across society;

- to decide how best society in general, and SCAA in particular, might support schools in the task of promoting pupils' spiritual, moral, social and cultural development.

The first part of the remit was designed to determine whether there is any truth in the belief, implicit in the question with which we started this chapter, that because we are a pluralist society we have no common values. It was thought by delegates that if it could be demonstrated once and for all that there *are* such values this would go a long way towards restoring teachers' confidence in this part of their work.

The second part of the remit was intended as a response to schools' perfectly reasonable complaint that the task of promoting pupils' spiritual, moral, social and cultural development could not be left solely to them; after all, promoting values in school is an uphill task if all a pupil needs to do is leave the school gates to see that these values do not always (or even often?) inform the behaviour of adults.

A number of organisations with a special interest in education and in young people, along with all the major religions and many other national organisations with a membership representative of the population at large, were invited to nominate members of the Forum. In the end the Forum had 150 members drawn from across society. These people were organised into ten groups all but one of which met three times[1], with conclusions from each meeting being passed to the other groups before the next meeting.

It did not take long for the 150 members of the Forum to decide that the idea that there are no shared values is nonsense. Almost as soon as they considered the question they came up with a number of values to which, they believed, everyone would subscribe, irrespective of their race, ethnic group, religion, age, gender or class. These values included friendship, justice, freedom, truth, self-respect and respect for the environment, amongst many others. How, they argued, could anyone of goodwill sincerely deny that they value such things? What is surprising, in fact, is not that there are values common to everyone, but that anyone should ever have thought otherwise.

One of the first objections that was made, in fact, to the values outlined in the Forum's statement, was that they were 'so obvious as to be anodyne', 'like apple pie and motherhood' and 'couched in terms that seem to be designed to avoid disagreement'. To all of these objections, however, there is only one answer: *of course*. So, for example, *of course* the Forum's statement is couched in terms designed to avoid disagreement: the Forum was not in the business of generating controversy, their aim was to draw up a set of values with which no-one of goodwill could disagree.

And *of course* the values, once stated, appear obvious, *of course* they smack of apple pie and motherhood: anything as fundamental as this, once stated, will appear obvious. This doesn't make it any less true. If the Forum had come up with anything controversial it would not have been doing its job.

And sometimes, of course, the obvious needs to be stated. It is the very obviousness of the values outlined in the Forum's statement that has, we suspect, made them invisible: over the last decade or so we have concentrated so hard – and for very good reasons – on recognising and celebrating difference, that we have become blind to the very samenesses that make the differences, in one very important sense, irrelevant. We should continue, of course, to recognise and celebrate difference, but we should also recognise and celebrate our common humanity.

That the values identified by the Forum are values upon which everyone of goodwill will agree was conclusively established by SCAA in a consultation that included a MORI omnibus poll of 1500 adults. Approximately 95% of those with whom we consulted agreed to the values outlined in the Forum's statement. This overwhelming consensus is empirical evidence for the claim that, despite the fact that we are a pluralist society, there is a robust set of values that are shared by all of us. The objection that these values are 'obvious' carries no weight at all.

Another type of objection often made to the Forum's statement of values is that very few people in society live up to these values and that this shows quite conclusively that these are *not* our values, whatever supposed consensus there is on them.

This objection, however, rests on a misunderstanding of what a value *is*. A value is precisely an *ideal*, something we *try* or *would like* to live up to. The fact that it is difficult, sometimes, to do what we believe we should do does not mean that we should lower our sights. It especially does not mean that we should lower them to reflect *actual* behaviour. This really would be a counsel of despair. As human beings it is in our nature to strive, to aim for goals that are, as yet, beyond us. It is in achieving these goals and setting ever new ones that our human dignity lies.

Behind this misunderstanding, however, there is an important point: the values that we profess are not always the values upon which we act. And if this is how we as adults behave then it is unsurprising that our children should follow our example. The fact that we claim these values as our own and yet often fail to live up to them shows that the values are more robust, in fact, than they may seem.

And if discussion of them, stimulated by the Forum's work, gives us reason to re-think our commitment to them and resolve to do better, we would be demonstrating to children our belief that, with self-discipline and perseverance, it *is* possible to resist the temptation always to take the easy way out. It will also provide for them the best possible example of how to increase self-respect. And if everyone in society, especially parents, employers and those in public life, were to do this, this would be the best possible way of supporting schools in the vital task of promoting pupils' spiritual, moral and social development.

Another form of objection to the Forum's statement of values was the claim that agreement has been achieved only by ignoring areas where there is massive disagreement. So, for example, some have argued that the Forum's statement simply ignores major disagreements on the sources of value, upon how we should behave, and in particular on how we should deal with moral conflict. Once again, in this objection, there is a misunderstanding and an important point to be made.

Those who bring this objection have misread the Forum's statement. In the preamble to that statement it says, quite explicitly, that the Forum agreed that there can be no agreement on either (a) the source of the values upon which we all agree or (b) the way in which these values should be applied in behaviour. This acknowledgement of the two areas of disagreement is important, precisely because if they are not understood there is a risk that the important areas of agreement will be undermined.

The Forum agreed, firstly, that there is no agreement on the source of value because those who believe in God believe that God is the source of all value, whilst those who do not believe in God think that the source of value lies in human nature. The resolution of this disagreement must await a proof, or disproof, of God's existence acceptable to both sides. Secondly, the Forum agreed that there is no agreement on the way in which the values should be applied in behaviour; some of those who embrace these values will argue that they ensure abortion is impermissible, others that they ensure abortion is permissible. The resolution of this disagreement must await the outcome of further debate.

And because the Forum did not even attempt to determine any ordering among the values they identified, it is quite clear that there will be situations in which more than one value applies and in which the values, therefore, might suggest two or more possibly incompatible courses of action. The Forum's work has not solved the problems of moral conflict.

The statement of values, then, is not the final word on morality. It is entirely neutral on the question of God's existence and on tough moral issues such as the abortion debate, and it does not provide us with an easy way of avoiding moral conflict. Why then, those who make this objection say, should we take any notice of it?

Again the answer is simple. Firstly it should be pointed out that the Forum did not set out to solve the problems which theologians and philosophers have grappled with for centuries. They had a simple brief – to decide whether there are any values that we all share – which they fulfilled very well. It would be unrealistic – to say the least – to expect the Government's curriculum advisers, and/or 150 people appointed by them, to solve these problems. It is unreasonable – to say the least – to interpret the Forum's statement as claiming that the Forum has done any of these things.

And to the question of why we should, therefore, think that the Forum has done anything useful, the only reply can be another question: must we solve these problems before we can say anything useful on morality? Do we have to know whether or not God exists before we can decide that truth, friendship and justice are valuable? Do we have to know the answer to the abortion question before we can say that human life and human choice are both valuable? Do we have to know the answer to every question of the form 'how should I act?' before we know that there are actions we *should* perform and actions that we should *not* and that the question of how we should act will always be determined, in some more or less complicated way, by our values?

The aim of the Forum was simply to discover whether there are any values that can justifiably be said, in our pluralist society, to be common to everyone, it was not to have the final word on morality. That their statement is not the final word on morality, therefore, is neither surprising nor problematic. But surely, it might be said, once we understand all the things that the Forum's statement will *not* do, the Forum's claim to have identified a set of values upon which we can all agree looks empty.

That it is not empty is illustrated by two considerations. First, the fact that there can be no productive disagreement without a fundamental level of agreement. Second, the question with which I started this chapter shows that there is a danger of our losing the very agreement that makes disagreement on moral truth potentially productive.

If there is no agreement on an issue, then there cannot be productive disagreement. If there is no recognition, for example, that we are talking about the same thing, then our disagreements on the nature of that thing, or on its source, or on its consequences become meaningless. Argument – the means by which human beings search for truth – is wholly dependent upon the existence of some basic agreement. We can potentially convince each other of our conclusions only if we can rely upon agreement on the premises and upon the steps of the argument itself. If there is no agreement on our starting point, and no agreement on the steps of the argument, then argument would be pointless and the truth would be forever beyond our reach.

Given this, the Forum's having identified a set of values upon which everyone can agree can be seen as the Forum's having identified a starting point for moral argument, the basis of agreement that makes possible productive disagreement about moral issues, a starting point recognition of which will put moral truth back on the agenda.

And that we are presently in danger of losing this starting point is shown by considering again the question with which we started this chapter. This question expresses doubt not about the *source* of the values that we share, nor about how they should be *applied in behaviour*, nor about how they should be *ordered*, but about *their very existence*. And this doubt, unlike the other doubts, threatens to undermine morality itself because it threatens the fundamental agreement that gives direction and purpose to moral disagreement.

It is our agreement on the values themselves that gives substance to the disagreements on their source, on the way in which they should be applied in behaviour and upon how they should be ordered. If we didn't agree on the fact that both human life and individual choice should be respected, then the abortion debate would be impossible. We disagree so violently *because* each side believes that the other's acceptance of the premise – that human life, or human choice, ought to be respected – should entail the other's acceptance of the conclusion. If we couldn't agree on the premises there would be no argument.

And of course, it isn't only argument on issues like abortion that is important, it is argument with those who believe, for example, that beating up someone with whom one disagrees is morally acceptable. It is arguably the false belief that because we are a pluralist society there are no common values that has led to the 'anything goes' view that permits abhorrent beliefs such as this. If, on the back of the belief that there are no common values, we lose our confidence in the claim that there are behaviours that are simply morally unacceptable, then how are we to argue convincingly with those whose values permit them to beat people up to signal disagreement? If we are ever to discover and/or convince others of the truth about what is right and wrong, then argument is necessary.

Agreement on values may not be the final word on morality, but in a society that has become blind to moral agreement it is of the utmost importance because not only does it lay the foundations for the acquisition of moral knowledge, it also tells us that there are ways in which we must *not* behave, it gives the lie to the socially disastrous – and false – view that 'anything goes'.

Finally the values outlined by the Forum have been objected to on the ground that schools already teach these values. This, of course, is right. Schools *do* already promote these values. Teachers cannot teach well without making it clear that they value, for example, truth, knowledge and wisdom and that it matters to them that their pupils should also come to value these things. Headteachers cannot do their job properly without making it clear that they value, for example, justice, fairness and collective effort for the common good. The Forum was given the task it was given not, as some of the more mischievous members of the press would have it, because schools are not already doing a good job, but because it was believed that, in the light of the false belief that because we are a pluralist society we have no common values, schools were having an uphill struggle. Schools need the active support of society if they are to succeed in the important task of promoting pupils' spiritual, moral, social and cultural development: the statement of values is not a birch with which society can beat schools, it is a tool that schools can use to elicit the help of society.

And this brings us, finally, to the second part of the Forum's remit, to the Forum's recommendations on how best society in general, and SCAA in particular, might support schools in this important work.

The Forum recommended that SCAA produce, for schools, guidance on the promotion of pupils' spiritual, moral, social and cultural development. This guidance, they said, should be flexible enough for schools to adapt it to their own circumstances, it should encourage rigour and a whole school approach and it should encourage partnership between schools, parents and the local community. The guidance, furthermore, should be supported by a booklet of case studies, a directory of resources, guidelines for community service and a glossary of the terms commonly used in this area. During consultation 73% of schools agreed that such guidance, supported by these materials, would be useful to them. SCAA is currently in the process of producing this guidance and its supporting material.

Importantly, however, this guidance will be built around the values outlined in the Forum's statement so that these values, the values shared by everyone of goodwill, will inform schools' promotion of pupils' spiritual, moral, social and cultural development. In addition to producing this guidance, however, SCAA will recommend to schools that they use the statement of values locally to:

- instil confidence in the existence and importance of shared values

- trigger debate about values (many schools will want to add to the values outlined in the Forum's statement)

- elicit support in the promotion of pupils' spiritual, moral, social and cultural development from parents, local employers and the local community generally.

SCAA, and its successor body, the Qualifications and Curriculum Authority (QCA), will play its part in supporting schools in this work by using the statement nationally in all these ways. We intend to trigger national debate about values, to elicit support for schools from major national employers', parents', governors' and teachers' organisations, and by these means to instil confidence, across society, in the fact that however different we are, our common humanity ensures that there are values we all share.

***

As a coda to this chapter the following pages present the SCAA's 'Preamble to the Statement of Values' and 'The Statement of Values'.

Note

1. The odd group – composed of representatives from the media – met only twice. It was interesting that the representatives from the media all came in order to report on what the Forum was doing rather than participate in the Forum's deliberations. We find this worrying: the media are, after all, part of society, they do not simply report on it.

The Preamble to the Statement of Values

The National Forum for Values in Education and the Community was set up by the School Curriculum and Assessment Authority to:

1. discover whether there are any values upon which there is common agreement within society;

2. decide how schools might be supported in the important task of contributing to pupils' spiritual, moral, social and cultural development.

The Forum identified a number of values on which members believed society would agree. Extensive consultation showed there to be overwhelming agreement on these values.

The second part of the remit was met by the recommendation that SCAA produce guidance for schools on the promotion of pupils' spiritual, moral, social and cultural development. This guidance, it was recommended, should be structured around the contexts of value, build upon current good practice, encourage rigour and a whole-school approach to work in this area and be supported by booklets of case studies, a directory of resources, a glossary of the terms commonly used in this area and guidelines for community service. It was also recommended that the guidance include suggestions on how the school might involve the local community in work in this area. SCAA was also asked to use the statement of values nationally to instil confidence, trigger debate and elicit support for schools in the vital task of promoting pupils' spiritual, moral and social development. This work is currently being planned.

It is important to note the following points:

- The remit of the Forum was to decide whether there are any values that are commonly agreed upon across society, not whether there are any values that *should* be agreed upon across society. The only authority claimed for these values, accordingly, is the authority of consensus.

- These values are not exhaustive. They do not, for example, include religious beliefs, principles or teachings, though these are often the source from which commonly-held values derive. The statement neither implies nor entails that these are the *only* values that should be taught in schools. There is no suggestion, in particular, that schools should confine themselves to these values.

• Agreement on the values outlined below is compatible with disagreement on their sources. Many believe that God is the ultimate source of value, and that we are accountable to God for our actions; others that values have their source only in human nature, and that we are accountable only to our consciences. The statement of values is consistent with these and other views on the sources of value.

• Agreement on the values is also compatible with different interpretations and applications of these values. It is for schools to decide, reflecting the range of views in the wider community, how these values should be interpreted and applied. So, for example, the principle 'we support the institution of marriage' may legitimately be interpreted as giving rise to positive promotion of marriage[1] as an ideal, of the responsibilities of parenthood, and of the duty of children to respect their parents.

• The ordering of the values does not imply any priority or necessary preference. The ordering reflects the belief of many that values in the context of the self must precede the development of the other values.

• These values are so fundamental that they may appear unexceptional. Their demanding nature is however demonstrated both by our collective failure consistently to live up to them, and the moral challenge which acting on them in practice entails.

Schools and teachers can have confidence that there is general agreement in society upon these values. They can therefore expect the support and encouragement of society if they base their teaching and the school ethos on these values.

Note

1. In British law, marriage is defined as 'the voluntary union for life of one man and one woman to the exclusion of all others'.

The Statement of Values

The Self

We value ourselves as unique human beings capable of spiritual, moral, intellectual and physical growth and development.

On the basis of these values, we should:

- develop an understanding of our own characters, strengths and weaknesses

- develop self-respect and self-discipline

- clarify the meaning and purpose in our lives and decide, on the basis of this, how we believe that our lives should be lived

- make responsible use of our talents, rights and opportunities

- strive, throughout life, for knowledge, wisdom and understanding

- take responsibility, within our capabilities, for our own lives.

Relationships

We value others for themselves, not only for what they have or what they can do for us. We value relationships as fundamental to the development and fulfilment of ourselves and others, and to the good of the community.

On the basis of these values, we should:

- respect others, including children

- care for others and exercise goodwill in our dealings with them

- show others they are valued

- earn loyalty, trust and confidence

- work co-operatively with others

- respect the privacy and property of others

- resolve disputes peacefully.

Society

We value truth, freedom, justice, human rights, the rule of law and collective effort for the common good. In particular, we value families as sources of love and support for all their members, and as the basis of a society in which people care for others.

On the basis of these values, we should:

- understand and carry out our responsibilities as citizens

- refuse to support values or actions that may be harmful to individuals or communities

- support families in raising children and caring for dependants

- support the institution of marriage

- recognise that the love and commitment required for a secure and happy childhood can also be found in families of different kinds

- help people to know about the law and legal processes

- respect the rule of law and encourage others to do so

- respect religious and cultural diversity

- promote opportunities for all

- support those who cannot, by themselves, sustain a dignified life-style

- promote participation in the democratic process by all sectors of the community

- contribute to, as well as benefit fairly from, economic and cultural resources

- make truth, integrity, honesty and goodwill priorities in public and private life.

The Environment

We value the environment, both natural and shaped by humanity, as the basis of life and a source of wonder and inspiration.

On the basis of these values, we should:

- accept our responsibility to maintain a sustainable environment for future generations

- understand the place of human beings within nature

- understand our responsibilities for other species

- ensure that development can be justified

- preserve balance and diversity in nature wherever possible

- preserve areas of beauty and interest for future generations

- repair, wherever possible, habitats damaged by human development and other means.

Chapter 2

Three proposals and a rejection

John White

This is a funny country. Nine years ago it introduced a National Curriculum based on traditional academic subjects with scarcely any provision for personal and social or civic education. These days its School Curriculum and Assessment Authority (SCAA) seems to spend most of its time bemoaning the fact that schools and teacher education colleges do next to nothing about moral and civic development.

The driving force here has been SCAA's Chief Executive, Dr Nick Tate. Although the backbone of the National Curriculum is rigidly academic, its aims do emphasise moral development among other kinds. How moral development is supposed to be promoted through the academic subjects has never been properly addressed, either in 1988 or since. But at least the authorities are now taking moral education very seriously. SCAA recently set up a Forum on Values in Education and the Community whose report was published in Autumn 1996.

Nick Tate's own ideas on the topic have been spelt out in a recent series of well-publicised speeches. His perception of the moral state of the British nation is not optimistic. In the past, at the heart of both home and school education was the transmission of a set of moral rules or precepts, like the Ten Commandments and the seven deadly sins. Now our society no longer has this framework. Whereas people used to believe in definite rights and wrongs, the dominant moral attitude today rests on an all-pervasive relativism – in Tate's interpretation of the term, the belief that morality is largely a matter of taste or opinion.

As for remedies, Nick Tate wanted his Forum to set out a list of core, universal values to which all schools will be committed. He would like to see how the whole curriculum can contribute to this end. In line with the connection he sees between moral decline and the erosion of a religious framework, he would like religious education to play a crucial role in re-establishing traditional moral qualities. In other recent speeches he has called for renewing traditional attachment to our national community and its cultural heritage, and expressed an interest in the role that personal and social education can play in civic education premised on such a community.

I very much welcome the new attention Nick Tate has been giving to moral and civic education, although I disagree with his diagnosis in many ways. There *is* a problem about moral attitudes in our society today, but it is not the one he picks out.

First, the claim that society is in moral decline. Not only Nick Tate thinks this. In the wake of certain horrific murders by children in the last few years media moralists have rushed to sound the tocsin. Some, like Nick Tate, have tied our moral woes to the loss of a religious framework. Is it true that we are in moral decline? If morality is as closely linked to religion as Nick Tate believes, perhaps it is. Certainly membership of Christian churches is in a spin-dive in Britain. Extrapolating from recent figures, I have calculated that, at a constant rate of decline, the churches will be completely empty somewhere between 2037 and 2076 (White 1995).

But why make moral values dependent on religion? Plato had well-justified doubts about this two and a half millenia ago in his dialogue the *Euthyphro*. Must it take forever for the message to get through? Let's give the religionists all the aces. OK, we'll agree with them – for now – that God exists. That's one fact. We'll agree that he's promulgated rules for human beings to follow – in the Judaeo-Christian case, Nick Tate's Ten Commandments. That's another fact. What have these facts to do with how we should morally behave? If someone commands me to keep my promises or not commit adultery, is this reason enough for me to do these things? Why should I obey orders without question? Suppose someone commands me to kill all my children, should I do so simply because he tells me to?

The Christian's traditional reply has been: 'Of course not. But God is different. God is good. The things which he enjoins are not like that. They could never be evil.'

Enter Plato from the *agora*. Are we to lead good lives just because God tells us to? Or because what God tells us to do is good? It seems to be the latter. But, if it is, there must be some *independent* standard of goodness – independent, that is, of God's commands. In which case morality could not rest on a religious basis, because underlying the alleged foundation is... morality!

Let's start again. We're talking about such things as not abusing people, telling the truth, helping others in distress, not breaking promises. It is not difficult to find a non-religious basis for these. Life would go badly for nearly all of us if there were no social constraints on people going about wounding or killing each other, lying and so on. If we were all made of indestructible metal, we might not need moral rules forbidding physical harm to people. But we are not. We are all horribly vulnerable and need protection from knives and fists and guns. Our basic moral rules reflect our human nature. (See Warnock, 1971, Ch. 2)

I will come back to this in a moment. We haven't finished with the question about whether our society is in moral decline. This sounds like a wholly empirical question – a matter of collecting the evidence to settle the issue one way or the other. But it isn't. We can't begin to answer it unless we agree what we take morality to be. I've just mentioned a number of what I called 'basic moral rules' – that one should tell the truth, avoid doing physical harm and so on. If we could draw up a definitive list of these, we could in principle collect data on the incidence of being truthful, not killing people, helping others in distress, etc. I say 'in principle', because once you've gone beyond ascertainable phenomena like murder rates, how you find out whether people are now more truthful or considerate is not so easy.

But can we draw up a definitive list of moral rules? Is there an agreed moral code? Whether some people would still see masturbation as a moral offence, I don't know. It certainly was when I was young, along with pre-marital sex and homosexual relationships. Today the battle lines are more likely to be drawn around the permissibility of abortion or euthanasia.

Would the moral code contain prohibitions on drug-taking and excessive use of alcohol or tobacco? Are these things *moral* defects? Again, this brings us back to what we mean by 'moral'. The term commonly refers to our behaviour towards other people. It's morally wrong to cheat them or to steal their property. If other people's harm is not at issue, are we still in moral territory? Think what has happened to the staples of sexual morality, just mentioned – to masturbation or premarital sex. Many today would argue that these aren't morally wrong if other people are not adversely affected. If we agree with them, should we say the same about the use of cannabis, heroin, beer and cigarettes? Is it only when junkies steal and mug to pay for drugs that this becomes a moral issue?

In one way, if there is uncertainty about what should be inside or outside a moral code, this is only grist to the mill of moral pessimists like Nick Tate. 'It wasn't like that in the old days. We knew where we were then. That's exactly why we need a Values Forum – to establish an agreed code of values for the future.' In other words, the perceived breakdown of consensus is itself used as evidence of a fall in moral standards. But should it be?

It might, after all, be a sign that people are becoming more reflective about how we should live together. If people no longer blindly do what conventional morality tells them, is this retrogression or advance?

This is perhaps the point to bring in what Nick Tate says about the dangers of relativism, in his eyes the dominant moral attitude today. What is relativism? Tate means by the term 'the view that morality is largely a matter of taste or opinion, that there is no such thing as moral error, and that there is no point therefore in searching for the truth about moral matters or in arguing or reasoning about it' (Speech at the SCAA Conference, 15 January 1996, para. 15).

Tate almost makes it seem as if people now treat moral values as matters of preference, like a choice between Heineken and Fosters, or between curry and fish and chips. Is there any evidence of this? Does he adduce any?

He says that relativism 'is widespread. A MORI poll in 1994 showed that 48% of 15-35 year olds did not believe that there were definite rights and wrongs in life, while 41% felt that morality always (not just sometimes) depended on the circumstances' (*ibid.*, para. 16).

Is this evidence of relativism, as Tate defines it? We would have to look further into how these poll results are to be interpreted. Take the first. Nearly half of the younger population does not believe that there are definite rights and wrongs. What does this mean? Does it mean that they don't believe that killing people, for instance, is something they should avoid? Or does it mean that they don't think killing is wrong *in every conceivable circumstance*? The difference is crucial. In the first case we would all have good reason to be very worried indeed. If half the upcoming generation doesn't care a fig about topping other people, we'd all better hire personal bodyguards. But if the second interpretation, which brings in different circumstances, is true, we may be able to relax. Is it *always* – in some absolute sense – wrong to kill people? But what about self-defence? Or in a just war? Or as a plotter against Hitler, like von Stauffenberg? Or in some cases of voluntary euthanasia? Perhaps the poll merely shows that the young now have a more *nuanced*, less black and white, attitude towards traditional moral rules – that they think things through more and see that there are justifiable exceptions to any moral rule, even the most basic.

All in all, Nick Tate hasn't convinced me that we are on a moral downward slope. I'd need firmer evidence before joining the hand-wringing or garment-rending brigade. I *do* believe, however, that in countries like ours we face a problem and that we need to take action to resolve it – but my diagnosis is different from Nick Tate's. The problem is not moral decline, but a certain *lack of confidence* about how we should behave and what we should believe.

We are living on something of a moral watershed. Nick Tate is right: old patterns are crumbling. It is not only a matter of religious decline and an increasing unwillingness to accept religious authority as backing for moral beliefs.

He is also right to highlight changing attitudes to our national community. In Britain's case, these have been intimately tied up, traditionally, with religion, that is, with Protestantism. After the union of England with Scotland which formed Britain in 1707, we grew used to thinking of Britain as a righteous, Christian country, at loggerheads with continental enemies, especially Catholic ones like the French (Colley, 1992). We thought of it, too, as the most civilised of nations, superior not only to other European countries, but also to the Indians and Africans and other peoples over which our great Empire came to rule. This traditional nationalism is now, mercifully, in terminal recession. It flares up from time to time – in the 1980s with the Falklands War and our righteous struggle against the foe, indeed a Catholic foe; and in the 1990s with our anti-EU posturings. But its number is almost up. Our traditional attachment to British national values, like our traditional attachment to the Church, is crumbling with the years.

Closely tied up with the nation and the church, two other traditional British institutions are also currently under threat. The first is the monarchy. The *mystique* of royalty, its intimate association with that shadowy entity the British nation, is dissolving fast. The second threat is to the traditional cult of work as the central pivot of a human life. This, like the monarchy, has been, historically, closely tied to religious values, especially, again, with Protestant values. The centrality of work in life over other activities and pursuits is now under growing challenge (White, 1997). People are not taking kindly to the fact that while working hours on the continent are falling, in Britain they are not. The place of work in our lives is coming up fast on the political agenda. I can scarcely ever open a copy of my daily newspaper, *The Independent*, without coming across headlines like '*Work can kill*' *warning* or *We must break our 45-hours-a-week habit*.

Nick Tate is right. Decreasing respect for traditional institutions *does* create a problem. But it's only a problem of decline if you think, as he does, that these old attitudes are worth preserving. The problem that I see is that we in Britain need a value-framework in which we can believe as confidently as, say 150 years ago, many of us believed in the Church, Nation, Queen and Hard Work. We are still searching for this. Assuming that we don't follow the Nick Tates back into the past, what should be our route into the future?

The issue is both about what the content of the value-framework should be and about how children should be inducted into it. I have three suggestions to make about these matters.

• It would be helpful if we could stop ourselves talking about morality and moral education as if these belonged to a part of our life rigidly separated off from the rest of it (Williams, 1985; Taylor, 1995). This way of thinking about them belongs to the tradition which I am suggesting we transcend. Central to this tradition is the notion of Duty. We divide our lives into one part dominated by our moral obligations, the things we morally ought to do; and another part where inclination, or pleasure, rather than duty comes into the story. The historical roots of this division lie in our Christian past; but its branches have spread over into a more secular age. Kant's moral philosophy based on his categorical imperative has been influential here.

It was Nietzsche in books like *The Genealogy of Morals* who first made people wonder whether morality was all it was made out to be. His present-day follower, Bernard Williams, adds analytic precision to the task of dynamiting what he calls in *Ethics and the Limits of Philosophy* the 'peculiar institution' of morality. Both writers see morality as we have come to understand it as a culturally bounded phenomenon, the now largely secular remnant of Christian commandments. Williams, in particular, points to the dominating role of obligation in the morality system, to the marginalising of other values which might guide us. Like Nietzsche, he urges us to look back to Greek ethical ideas for inspiration. Traditional morality has been built around *rules* – originally God's commandments, later secularised versions of these. We think of morality as a code of things we ought and ought not to do. The Greeks thought of how human beings should live in terms of *virtues* of character – personal qualities like courage, which regulates our fear-responses; self-control, which sifts out appropriate from inappropriate expressions of anger; and temperance, which strikes a similar mean in the way we handle our bodily appetites for food, drink and sex (and, in our modern age, we should add drugs, including alcohol and tobacco).

A major step forward would be to enlarge our conception of values-education so as to include cultivating the virtues, like generosity, courage, friendliness, patience as well as inducting into rules against such things as stealing, killing, lying and breaking promises.

In fact, when you think about it, if you take the rule against killing, there's not much to do here in the way of inducting children into it. By this, I don't mean that the prohibition against killing is not important. Quite the opposite. It is *so* fundamental as to be utterly taken for granted. Killing a human being belongs to the realm of the unthinkable. With few or no exceptions children don't need moral education programmes in order to learn not to do it.

This gives us a useful way of thinking about values education. Some ethical considerations, like the one just mentioned, should be seen as embedded in the very framework of a civilised life. Reject them and you reject civilisation. You outlaw yourself from your community. Not killing is one example, so is not injuring, so is not stealing.

Other ethical considerations have to do with learning to make appropriate responses and have appropriate feelings. These are the virtues. All of us are born with or come to acquire emotions and desires, like fear, anger, thirst, hunger, love of company, feelings of self-worth. We need to learn how to handle these appropriately. Aristotle's *Nicomachean Ethics* is still an excellent guide into this process of habituation and to the gradually expanding role that reason comes to play in the process.

Somewhere between the two types of consideration – the framework prohibitions and the virtues – are rules against lying, promise-breaking, not helping people in distress, being unfair. These also belong to the very structure of civilised life, yet they also require habituation. Like the virtue of temperance, which regulates our bodily appetites, or the virtue of self-control, which does the same for anger, they control the temptations, or inclinations, we all have when we are young to follow easier paths. In the case of lying, being unfair etc. the inclination in question is usually putting our own interests first and not considering other people's. Education *is* necessary here – unlike with killing: we do not have to learn painfully to cope with our inclinations to kill or maim people. It is perhaps best to see learning not to lie, not turning away from those in need etc. as part of acquiring the virtue of concern for other people's well-being. Rather than laying down these things as mere rules, it would be better to develop children's sympathetic imagination, so that they come to feel how dreadful it must be like to be at the receiving end of an injustice or a breach of trust. That way they should, we may hope, feel less and less tempted to overstep these marks.

So the first suggestion as to ways forward would be to enlarge our conception of what moral or values education might involve, so as to include habituation into the virtues as well as learning familiar moral rules. Where possible, the distinction between virtues and rules could well be eroded in the way just mentioned.

• The second suggestion brings us back to what I was saying about the need for *confidence*. (I am indebted here, once again, to Williams, 1985. See pp. 170-1). There is nothing recondite or especially problematic about the ethical considerations mentioned so far. If religion is crumbling away as a justifying framework for morality, we should not think of ourselves as in some terrible intellectual limbo, not knowing which way to turn, looking to Kant or Mill or Sartre or Freud or Marx to help us sort out whether there is some objective basis to our moral beliefs, or whether, given that God is dead, what we choose as the values by which to live is up to us. I know very well that this is the message that religionists tend to come out with: that once you leave the solid territory of religion you fall into a morass of doubt, uncertainty and despair. But it is *not* like that. How many of us go around radically uncertain whether in general (i.e. leaving out exceptional cases) it is wrong to kill or inflict grievous bodily harm? If we are to lead a civilised life at all, we *know* that such things should not be permitted, that they are beyond the pale. The same with lying, breaking promises and the rest. If human beings were different – if, as I said earlier, they were made of indestructible metal so that they could never be killed or injured, or if they didn't plan ahead so that broken promises could not interfere with what they had in mind to do – then things would be otherwise. We wouldn't need these rules. But we all have an implicit understanding of the kinds of creatures we are; given this, it should make perfectly good sense to us that, if we are to have a minimally civilised life, these kinds of things must be insisted on.

We shouldn't, therefore, be a prey to radical doubt about such matters. We need confidently to embrace these values ourselves; and, as parents and teachers, confidently to instil them in our children.

Similar points can be made about virtues like temperance, courage, friendliness, generosity, patience, good-humouredness etc. There is nothing deeply problematic about the fact that human beings have appetites for food, drink, sex. We all know this. We also know that, unlike other animals, we cannot rely on instinctual mechanisms to control these appetites. We know that children – like all of us – are all tempted to eat too much on occasion, or eat the wrong things, or eat the right things but in the wrong places. We also know that they need constant guidance in their early years so that they come to do what is appropriate – good for their health, suitable to the circumstances. We know that habituation in the virtue of temperance is necessary if they are to flourish, if they are to lead fulfilling lives. The same is true for the other virtues.

So about instilling the virtues, too, there should be no room for scepticism or vacillation. We should go ahead confidently building up these dispositions in children.

• The third and last suggestion about the way forward springs out of what I have said about the virtues and about not making a wall of steel in our lives between our moral duties and our inclinations.

One way of looking at the connections between the two is to consider whether control of one's bodily appetites is a *moral* virtue. One reason for uncertainty about this might be that this virtue is primarily *self-regarding*, whereas morality is often taken to be about one's duties to others. It's *my* flourishing, *my* happiness that is at stake if I don't handle these appetites successfully. Agreed, other people may well be adversely affected if I don't: those who love me, victims of my untamed sexual appetite or drug addictions, etc. Temperance is important primarily for my own well-being, but also for others'.

The third suggestion is that, in reviewing the moral life and the requirements of moral education, we should put the pupil's own flourishing much more at the centre of things than has been traditional, especially in the religious morality which we are now finally shaking off (White, 1990, Chs 2-4).

A difficulty has been that the religious tradition has bequeathed us no real picture of what a personally fulfilled life could be like except in terms of devotion to God and one's moral duties. Apart from this there are only the pleasures and temptations of our animal nature – held to be a common but false picture of a happy life, from which Duty alone can rescue us. As the religious view has waned over the twentieth century, not surprisingly the pagan conception of a happy life which it rejected has come into prominence. Not that, in our society today, people have gone overboard for selfish hedonism and have jettisoned all the old morality. Not at all. What I suspect has happened in a lot of cases is that people still have something like the traditional moral beliefs that they shouldn't harm others in the usual ways – lying, stealing etc. – but that since most of these are about things to *refrain* from, it's perfectly possible to live out one's life within these moral rules, yet spend an enormous proportion of it on one's own pursuits. Paradoxically, it is through their attachment to something not so far removed from traditional morality that some people in our society – how many, I don't know – seem to enjoy, strive for or dream of some version of the old religious view of the *dolce vita* of physical comforts and pleasures – sex, suntan and Sangria, electronic paradises, nice houses and nice gardens, coming up on the Lottery, villas in Spain or the South of France.

The main task for education has nothing to do with entrenching our entrenched morality still further. We are perennially tempted to take this route, but it leads nowhere. It simply deepens the over-moralisation that Britain – along with some other countries – has suffered from for many a century and the over-hedonisation which has afflicted it throughout the twentieth. The main task for education is to broaden young people's conceptions of what their own happiness or fulfilment might consist in. Not *just* this. For a merely intellectual aim is not enough. It must be accompanied by a form of upbringing which gives them the qualities of character, the sources of inner strength, to sustain them in their quest for a flourishing life.

To repeat. The religious-moral tradition from which we are emerging has left us with insufficient vision of what a fulfilled human life could consist in once the religious wraps are off. *This* is where the educational effort needs to go – in giving pupils a rounded picture of their *own* well-being. Part of this will certainly have to do with the animal enjoyments at which the religious tradition turned up its nose. The sexual liberation that a later generation than my own – unfortunately for me – has experienced has been a massive, if not wholly unalloyed, contribution to human welfare. But there is just so much else that can help make a happy life – gardening, enjoying the countryside, travel, the arts, co-operating with others on all sorts of tasks, political involvement, meditation, raising a family, sports, socialising...

Like me, I imagine you have sometimes had the thought that there are so many unexplored delights open to you that ten lifetimes would not be enough to experience them all. As a young person you backpack to Venice, discover Tintoretto and find the whole world of Italian renascence painting opening up to you. You read some stories by Chekhov and ditto for Russian literature. A chance visit to Exmoor unlocks the charms of rural beauty and solitude. And so on. For lucky ones like us, life is full to overflowing : even if we have few means, all we need at minimum is a good public library and some time to ourselves. It is hard for us to imagine that, for others, life is not at all overflowing. Its circle of enjoyments is small and boredom is always near.

The first task of education is to fill young people's horizons with multiple, and multiplying, visions of how they can fill their lives. Maybe this is one of the aims of the English National Curriculum; but if it is, those who have imposed it on the schools have not been letting on.

If I could redesign our National Curriculum, I would build in a new form of assessment at age sixteen. This would be the Fullness of Life Test. Feeling that twenty lifetimes would not be enough to drain life dry would merit a distinction grade; eighteen lifetimes, a merit, and so on down.

My third suggestion has been that when we think about values education, we move the pupil's own well-being much more to the centre of the stage. Enriching his or her personal life becomes a major aim. Does this mean we are playing down a more specifically *moral* education? In one way, not at all. I am not at all suggesting that we bring up our children to be a nation of egoists, concerned only with their own fulfilment at the expense of other people's. A personally flourishing life should not be conflated with a selfish one. This thought is a legacy from our religious past and we would do well to abandon it. Many, perhaps most, of the activities which constitute our own personal well-being inextricably help to further other people's goals as well as our own. Think of the items in the list I just reeled off: sexual activities, sports, country pursuits, working with others on some co-operative task, enjoying artistic and academic activities, raising a family, socialising ... We will not get very far with these things if we think of ourselves as social atoms. They all involve participation with others at point after point.

We need to bring children up to think of their own happiness as closely bound up with the happiness of others. For this, as I say, we need to enlarge their horizons about what such a mutually fulfilling life could consist of. This notion, that one's own flourishing should be thought of as inseparable from that of others in one's community, is, once again, an ancient Greek idea. It is poles apart from the dualist notion that puts Moral Duty on one side and Personal Inclination on the other.

If we *have* to be traditionalists about moral education, why go for something as recent and jejune as Christian morality? Why not push further back – say, to pre-Christian Athens?

Chapter 3

Can Education Be Moral?

Mary Midgley

There does seem to be something odd – even comical – about the idea of moral education – something that seems to set it apart from other aspects of education. When the British Education Secretary called on schools in 1994 to 'teach children the difference between right and wrong', many people felt this oddness. Teaching *that* particular difference didn't seem to be quite like teaching other kinds of difference, such as the difference between wasp-stings and bee-stings, or between Hungary and Romania. Gilbert Ryle once wrote an article called 'On Forgetting the Difference Between Right and Wrong' to bring out that this would be a strange kind of forgetting ... But you can forget the difference between wasp and bee-stings quite easily.

We will come back to Ryle's serious point presently, but it may be best to deal first with a smaller matter about the language. This talk about 'teaching the difference between right and wrong' is probably not intended to have its full literal meaning. It isn't a matter of explaining this huge difference in the first place to someone who doesn't know that it exists at all. That kind of ignorant person would presumably be like someone who doesn't know the difference between black and white, which means someone who was blind and without visual imagery. But anyone who was as lost as that morally would presumably be a very extreme psychopath, and it probably wouldn't be much use talking to them.

Moralists like Mr. Patten are not usually talking about these rare psychopaths. They are talking about large numbers of quite ordinary people who (they think) misplace the moral borderline. These people may, for instance, believe that it's all right to steal or play truant, or that it's wrong to report offences to the police. But they do not necessarily approve of murder. They may be much like everybody else on other moral topics. They have, in fact, got a general moral apparatus in their heads for making these distinctions and they do make them, but they make some of them wrongly. They need, then, to be taught certain particular Virtues so that they will get these particular distinctions right.

Now the teaching of virtues is not a new project. It was high on the curriculum of the ancient Greek Sophists. Protagoras in particular promised to teach his pupils virtue for a fixed price and guaranteed to repay the fee if the treatment was not successful. 'My young friend,' says Protagoras in Plato's dialogue, 'if you become my disciple, you will find that on the very first day you will go home a better man than you came; on the second day the result will be the same, and each succeeding day will be marked by the same improvement' (Plato, *Protagoras*, 318a).

Nobody, it seems, ever did sue Protagoras for non-delivery. (As that skilled public-relations expert had calculated, his pupils were not attracted by the prospect of coming into court to prove that they still remained vicious). All the same, there is surely something very odd about the Protagorean claim, something which bothered Socrates in much the same way that John Patten's claims bother us. Socrates attacked Protagoras by entangling him in logical contradictions about the idea of teaching virtue and concluded, somewhat paradoxically, that virtue simply can't be taught at all. But this is paradoxical because it surely looks as though Socrates himself did in some sense set out to teach virtue, and indeed as if his followers thought that he succeeded.

This whole situation, then, is a bit more complicated than it looks. Wild and simple claims, such as those made by Protagoras and Mr. Patten, cram the intellectual and the moral aspects of life together far too crudely. They suggest that virtue is just one more school subject, a set of facts and methods which can be handed out to pupils, like any other, in the classroom and tested by examination. (Question 3: Is Theft Wrong? . . .) Against this, we want to protest at once *that people can only become better by their own efforts.* Other people can't make them better. We want to say that the only possible scene for this struggle is the free choice of the individual concerned. And we also feel that this struggle hasn't much connection with learning new facts or new methods of thought.

Yet clearly this is not quite the whole story. Other people's influence does make a difference to the drama, and grasping new facts and new methods can also enter into it. For instance, when we discover that other people actually mind how we treat them – which is a fact – and again, that there do exist alternative possible ways of treating them – which is also a fact – these facts can radically change our attitudes. For instance, public attitudes in Britain both to domestic violence and to the oppression of colonial peoples have changed deeply in our lifetime as a result of some dim, dawning recognition of this kind of fact.

If we do absorb large new facts like these, we usually also need to develop new ways of thinking about them. In fact, at this stage, intellectual effort to understand the changed situation does become necessary. And that effort can often need help from outside – help which is, in effect, teaching, though it need not officially be so called. This kind of painful thinking is often simply too hard to perform quite on one's own. At this point, books as well as people may well be one's teachers, and it would be very odd to be so insistent on independence as to reject their influence. There is today a whole area of counselling and therapy to supplement these unofficial influences. The sense in which this can be called teaching is complicated. But it certainly is something extraneous to us, not an assertion of pure independence.

This point that outside help may be needed may seem an obvious one. But it still needs making today because, since the Enlightenment, some of our moral views have become so individualistic – so obsessed with protecting individual freedom from outside interference – that they have tended to isolate each person in an unbreathable moral vacuum in a way that paralyses action. This isolationist strand of thought has stemmed partly from Social Darwinist insistence on commercial freedom but more deeply from Nietzsche. It was dominant in Existentialism and it seems to rule also in some postmodern moral views. When this kind of moral solipsism is around, we need to say that humans are social animals. Their morality, like every other aspect of their lives, has to be formed co-operatively. That co-operation doesn't displace each individual's own struggle. It supplements it. But both are equally necessary. That is why there is room for some kind of teaching.

Change

Perhaps, then, there is a genuine connection between the intellectual and the moral aspect of life, making a genuine space for some kind of teaching at that point. Though this link is far more subtle than our hopeful prophets suggested, it does exist, because hard, co-operative thinking is needed in order to make moral changes. This is a fact which British anti-intellectualism prefers not to know, but it is true all the same. Except in the most stagnant cultures, thought is constantly needed for morals. Conceptual frameworks have to keep growing. And this growth is, of course, needed particularly badly in changing societies, societies where the force of custom is shaken and traditional restraints have been weakened.

However, moralising is always out of date. Societies are usually preoccupied with denouncing the faults of their predecessors. We keep fighting the last battle. On this principle, we still tend today to preach individualism and attack the faults of limited, stagnant, rule-bound cultures. We still repeat, in fact, the protests made by people like Nietzsche and Kierkegaard against the stagnation of European society in the late nineteenth century. It is of course true that small stagnant cultures have their own characteristic vices. They are often stifling, boring and frustrating. They do, however, tend to protect people's everyday life to some predictable extent. Putting it crudely, offenders in such societies tend to know that they are offending and also tend to get found out.

By contrast, our societies today are mobile, interconnected and fluid to an extent that is quite unparalleled in history. All of them are changing fast. People in each of them are aware of a multitude of other societies quite unlike their own that exist around them and can be reached. This fluidity means that unthinking conformity gets harder and harder. Thought really is needed to see what we ought to do.

In very static cultures, people really may get on well enough without much thought by simply following example. But in times of change like ours, not only does etiquette give way but people often really do not know what they ought to do. The present confusion of commercial morality is only one of many obvious examples. There is then usually an increase in what are by anyone's standards seriously destructive actions – killings, injuries, demolitions, arson. Not only are dreadful things done, but people are no longer sure just why they should not be done. The reasons that used to be taken for granted have been forgotten, or if they are remembered they no longer seem adequate. The conceptual floor-boards have to be taken up and ruling moral ideas re-examined.

The role of philosophy

Now this was the kind of essentially practical emergency that first produced serious, full-scale moral philosophising in Europe. In Greece, and above all in Athens, it arose, not in the full intellectual flowering of the successful Periclean age, but later, when things were unmistakably starting to fall to pieces. The reason why people listened to Socrates and Plato was that they were already badly shaken by upsets to their whole conceptual system – upsets which were primarily practical rather than theoretical. Moral philosophy didn't actually originate as a speculative exercise that was later applied to practical use, any more than modern physics did. (Galileo was an engineer working on the flight of cannon-balls). But in order to meet these practical emergencies, both physics and philosophy had to stand right back from those immediate practical problems. They needed to take up more distant viewpoints and look at a much wider subject-matter. It is that kind of detachment – that gap between immediate needs and the theoretical viewpoint – which produces the paradox, the sense that thought both is relevant to our practical attitudes and is somehow too remote to be much help with them.

Individualism

As I've suggested, this shake-up of tradition typically occurs when smaller, more rule-bound societies dissolve and get merged in larger, more mobile ones. Today, this is, of course, happening in spades all over the world. All contemporary societies, even the most protected, are changing fast. This means that the kind of unthinking moral conformity which people have used throughout most of human history constantly gets more difficult. Thought really is needed to see what one ought to do.

On top of this, however, there is at present a positive propaganda campaign against traditional submission to order. Both from the right and from the left, Western culture preaches individualism, making personal freedom itself a central ideal and calling for constant innovation. People don't only find themselves isolated from their traditional backgrounds and forced into competition, they are also told that they *ought* to be innovative, independent and competitive, that this is the way to adapt to a fluid situation. In official Western theory as well as in practice, the social aspect of morality has been considerably neglected – indeed, it has often been treated as something disreputably close to Communism. So it surely ought to be no surprise to anyone if crime and irresponsibility increase.

The question, however, is of course not just about causes and who is to blame. It concerns what we can do about this increase. Now the right-wing answer to this question recommends 'teaching them a lesson' by stern deterrent punishment, if necessary involving lots of boiling oil. This notion of how moral education works is very old and it has been most thoroughly tried out in practice. The trouble is that it doesn't actually work. Disappointingly, it turns out that 'the difference between right and wrong' cannot be effectively taught by this method. The threat of punishment may frighten people, but they often get used to it and go on as usual, as people threatened with hanging for sheep-stealing still stole sheep.

Moreover punishment, however frightful, does not, of itself, have any tendency to inculcate better practical attitudes. It won't teach people respect for the feelings of others or willingness to spare their property. The reason why it doesn't is that those attitudes are – fairly obviously – quite complex. They are not the sort of simple habit that can be taught to rats or pigeons by giving them electric shocks. Nor are they patterns which could be programmed into computers. Moral attitudes of this kind involve a great deal more than the fear of being punished. They usually need to be caught from people who have already got them, people whom one respects and with whom one can identify. That process is necessarily slow and not very articulate. That is why people growing up always absorb their first moral attitudes unconsciously from those around them.

These attitudes involve deeply ingrained habits of *attending* to differences between different ways of acting – differences such as, for instance, the difference between hurting people's feelings and not hurting them. Grasping this difference is not just learning that these two things are encouraged or not encouraged or are called *right* and *wrong*. And the reason why – as Ryle pointed out – these differences are not easily *forgotten* is that, once one has seen the point of them, they take their place as central factors in one's whole habitual attitude to choice.

Punishment can only help this process where it is seen and accepted as a comment from people whom one already respects, inside groups with which one can identify. That can happen much more easily with parents than it can with schools, which is why there are limits to what schools can be expected to do. It also happens more easily with schools than with the law. The trouble with judicial punishment is that it is usually administered by people outside the group in which the offenders mostly live. If those offenders have already begun to feel that their own group is alien to the wider society, then legal punishment is likely to strike them either as an accident or simply as a hostile act from an enemy. They may then quite easily take pride in ignoring it.

Where that kind of respect and identification is missing, then, offenders usually receive punishment like bad weather, simply as bad luck, reflecting that they will be more careful not to get caught next time. By contrast, the process of real attitude-change is much more like planting trees or tending a garden than it is like programming or conditioning. People who expect school-teachers, rather than prisons, to reform the offending young do no doubt sometimes have this kind of gardening process in mind. They may think of 'teaching the difference between right and wrong' rather more realistically as involving a combination of example and advice, rather than just as drilling in something like the difference between wasp-stings and bee-stings.

Undoubtedly, good school-teachers do often manage to do a lot of this gardening, in spite of the countless difficulties of their lot. Counsellors and therapists may do it too. And it's important to notice here that effective counselling of this kind is never going to be what is proudly called 'non-directive'. The idea that neutrality is possible is just self-deception. All professionals, however professional they may try to be, have their own moral attitudes. Communicating these attitudes is always a necessary part of any teaching process, even teaching the multiplication table. Attempts to hide or neutralise them can only result in confusion. The pupil or client doesn't have to accept those attitudes, and may indeed react against them. But they have to be there, perceptibly on offer. And in so far as they are offered to the client or pupil, some kind of teaching is necessarily going on.

Example and advice, then, do have a teaching function at this stage. But example and advice alone aren't enough once you are teaching a child that is old enough to think for itself. There has to be serious thought as well, thought which involves explicit discussion. Questions have to be answered. Objections have to be taken seriously. In times of change, this interactive stage of moral education can't be avoided.

The fear of dialogue

Discussion, however, scares right-wing theorists. They see that discussion has to start by positively inviting moral criticism, and that the first critical move will nearly always be a destructive one. Many people, of course, only make one such critical move in their lives – the one that takes them from their parents' position to that of their peer-group, where they follow whatever honour-code is locally going. Others, going a little farther, pick up some simple moral theory which looks like a useful justification for change – hedonism, egoism, relativism, nihilism, subjectivism, immoralism, Social Darwinism, general scepticism or (more usually) a jumble of bits and pieces from all these. Socrates got executed for 'corrupting the youth' because he had encouraged a lot of young people to start thinking and arguing destructively in this sort of way. And many of them had not bothered to go any further. It is possible, indeed, that Socrates was rather naive about this. As Plato seems finally to have concluded, something more positive may indeed be needed.

But there is nothing to stop anyone going further. Reasoning about morals is indeed one of those courses of action that need to be carried through properly; they are only dangerous if you stop halfway and don't see where they have taken you. (A little thinking is a dangerous thing ...) Thus, Benjamin Franklin, as a young man, took up with immoralism and published a pamphlet to prove 'that nothing could possibly be wrong in the World, that Vice and Virtue were empty Distinctions, no such Thing existing'. (There was, in fact, strictly no difference between right and wrong.)

His friends were much impressed with his reasoning. But Ben was then annoyed to find that two of these friends took his arguments seriously. They now refused to pay him back quite large sums of money which he had lent them . . . He also noticed that he himself had been behaving meanly to his girlfriend. At this point, Ben says, 'my Pamphlet appeared now not so clever a Performance as I once thought it, and I doubted whether some Error had not insinuated itself unperceived into my Argument . . . I grew convinced that Truth, Sincerity and Integrity in Dealings between Man and Man were of the utmost Importance to the Felicity of Life.'

That experience showed Ben where he had got to. Without a difference between right and wrong, his life didn't make sense any longer. He didn't like this, and accordingly revised his reasoning. When he asked himself where he would now put that difference, he found quite good reason for putting it, on that matter, where it had been before, though on other matters he later saw reason to shift it. He ended, not by ditching morality, but by making a shift within it to emphasis on different standards, different claims.

This kind of progress through extreme positions to more subtle ones is a perfectly normal and proper response to a clash of values, even in stable times. In an age of violent change, when there simply is no single, solid unquestioned framework to shelter in, it may well be the only way forward to some kind of tenable position. We can't put ourselves back into an age of monolithic moral simplicity. (We wouldn't like it if we could and indeed there have been few such ages.) Instead, we can rethink our values, noticing where they clash, where they still seem to be right and where changes of priority are actually called for.

Right-wing theorists share a mistake about this with the violent rebels who confront them. They suppose that there are only two choices. We must either swallow traditional morality whole or else drop it altogether. That assumption leaves no room for morality to grow. But we know that morality does grow, that it *has* grown in the past and that it is bound to go on growing in the future. Our business is to contribute to that growing by trying to see better the wider spectrum of possible ideals, standards and values which lies beyond the narrow choices currently before us.

The simple moral dualism that sees only two choices springs partly from the mere habit of feuding – from always seeing issues as fights between Them and Us. But it arises also from sheer lack of practice in reasoning. People who are used to seeing every argument treated as a quarrel find it really hard to suspect that more than two possibilities can exist at all. To bring this idea into perspective calls for serious discussion.

Discussing – serious, open-minded discussing rather than just disputing – is not easy. It is something that people need to learn to do while they are still young and flexible. As is recognised in almost every civilised country other than our own, that discussion is inevitably philosophical. Philosophy, in fact, is not a luxury. At least in confusing times like ours, philosophy is an unavoidable necessity. It will be done, well or badly, in any case. Even the individualistic, monetarist views which now prevail are themselves quite recent contributions to philosophy, though they are bad ones. There is a great deal to be said for finding better ones instead.

Chapter 4

Fabulously Absolute

Paul Standish

'The preoccupation with self-satisfaction and the infantilising of our images of human life that result from consumerism, and from pop culture consumerism in particular, must be one of the conference's main concerns.'[1] Addressed to the conference 'Education for Adult Life: the spiritual and moral development of young people', Nick Tate's words expressed sentiments that were widely shared: technological advances and a money-centred value system increase materialistic expectations and selfish values; marriage breakdown, geographical mobility, changes in communications and the mass media lead to the fragmentation of the family and the collapse of historic communities; the spiritual is marginalised. What can be said about the kinds of moral breakdown that are brought about?

Sometimes moral breakdown can be seen in relief, and our moral lives can be better understood, when we look at extreme circumstances where things have gone drastically wrong. There are examples in fiction where writers have focused on catastrophic circumstances precisely for such a purpose, *Lord of the Flies* being one of the most famous. In this chapter I begin by looking at a story that does just this, a short story called *Lot* by Ward Moore, first published in 1953.

The scene is suburban Los Angeles in the wake of a nuclear attack on the city. Pittsburg has already been devastated. Residents have been advised by the radio to stay in their homes and to remain calm. But the streets fill with cars and the routes out to the north of the city are jammed in a mass exodus. There are fights at petrol stations, shootings, police patrols are powerless. As communities fragment, concern narrows to the family. There is no law now but the law of survival. Truly awful though things are, Mr Jimmon takes some satisfaction in the way he is coping. The car has been properly prepared, the essentials have been loaded, he is ready to go. Of course, the youngest child has to be made to leave the beloved dog behind, his wife has to be made to forget about contacting the neighbours. As they join the heavy traffic, the three children in the back squabble as if with the irritability of a long, hot vacation trip in a crowded car. Mrs Jimmon points out that there are some 'awfully nice hotels' in the area they can stay in.

As he drives relentlessly away from the city, Mr Jimmon ponders the fate of his family. His younger son, now nine years old, will soon lose the 'tags and scraps of progressive schooling' to become primitive, superstitious and savage, like all the other children of his age. His older son will go wild in another sense: 'His values were already set; they were those of television, high school dating, comic strips, law and order. Released from civilization, his brief future would be one of guilty rape and pillage until he fell victim to another youth or gang bent the same way.' Whatever semblance of morality these children have acquired, it won't be enough for the changes they now face.

But what of his wife? Surely she knows what's right and what's wrong. She has lived her life by a rigid code: 'honour thy father; iron rayon the wrong side; register and vote; avoid scenes; only white wine with fish; never rehire a discharged servant'. These precepts she has followed dutifully, playing the role of mother and home-maker; all are equally serviceable in the comfort and propriety of her life in suburban Los Angeles. They are the signposts in the story she lives by. Now that this world has gone, she will disintegrate and perish quickly.

And the consumerism infecting her children's lives is implicit in the superficial world of comfort and respectability that Mrs Jimmon cannot leave behind. Its standards and decency are achieved with an erosion of the contours of moral geography, where rules for living guide one equally in the way to treat one's parents and the way to iron one's clothes. Her moral failure is like a residue of that inability of very young children to distinguish between the different contexts in which 'right' and 'wrong' are used, a self-indulgent immaturity characteristic perhaps of the society she clings to.

Such is the life they have left behind them. Mr Jimmon's elation at the way he has risen to the crisis, his liberation by the cataclysm, hints at escape from a humdrum existence in a safe job, an empty marriage, a moribund society. Only his fourteen year-old daughter, calm and composed, seems to share with him some intimation of what is really happening, how things will never be the same again: 'Only Erika was a true Jimmon. Made in my own image,' he thought pridelessly.' For the others there is really no hope.

When they stop for petrol and the rest room, Mrs Jimmon tries to telephone the neighbours; Mr Jimmon sends the boys into the shop to buy sweets. Then he does the only practical thing and, asking his daughter to get into the car, abandons the others and drives away.

It is in the multiple significances of the title of the story that the indictment is most telling. Theirs has been the society of plenty, material possessions in abundance. Now this is their lot, the fate of American prosperity. And Mrs Jimmon is Lot's wife: unable to refrain from casting her eyes back at the fallen city, at the life they have come from, she is transfixed and incapacitated for the life ahead. Lot's daughters get him drunk and, in his stupor, sleep with him; Mr Jimmon escapes chaos and destruction, we are to imagine, for survival with his daughter.[2] And here the implications become harder to fathom. Even if we can countenance Mr Jimmon's pragmatic and realistic decision to abandon the hopeless members of his family – for survival, the absolute value, he says – his success, it seems, is irrevocably poisoned. It is clear at least, as Mr Jimmon and Erica realise, that whatever bonds held their society together have been torn apart, and little hope, though they may *not* see this, that practical resourcefulness alone can renew them. The shadow of incest here hints at a darker side to family values, how these things are more complicated than we like to assume.

The story also raises important questions about following rules. As Mrs Jimmon fails to see, some rules are clearly moral and some seem more like matters of taste or etiquette: sometimes, as SCAA put it, 'the word 'wrong' will refer only to socially unacceptable behaviour (it is wrong to poke your tongue out), while at other times a moral absolute is involved' (SCAA, 1995, p. 5). There is a difference between how you treat your mother and how you iron rayon. (Who wears rayon now anyway?) What does it mean to say that some *moral* rules are absolute? For it is this claim that is at the heart of the condemnation of moral relativism in all its forms. Mrs Jimmon is an absolutist, but an absolutist of an absurdly crude kind. It would manifestly be wrong to link anything like her simplistic 'morality' with the views we are addressing, but what *is* meant by absolutism is very much our concern. 'Schools should be expected to uphold those values which contain moral absolutes' (*ibid.*) – we need to get clearer about what this amounts to.

For a start, what is absolutism being opposed to? It is clearly being opposed to relativism. Relativism, Tate claims, assumes that 'morality is largely a matter of taste or opinion, that there is no such thing as moral error and that there is no point therefore in searching for the truth about moral matters'. If this is relativism, we can say (with Tate) that it has stifled debate, created a national embarrassment about questions of value, and led to confusion over the virtue of tolerance with misplaced anxiety about giving offence. Ironically, such views are often (and perhaps unwittingly) held with what is in effect an absolutist commitment – to freedom, autonomy, equality, and respect for individuals. It is true that there is a familiar contemporary set of attitudes to the effect that morality is just a matter of taste or opinion, and there are sound arguments against these attitudes. But by characterising these attitudes, or the position that overarches them, as relativism, the debate is oversimplified. Relativism here is a matter of people saying that things all come down to personal opinion. Such a position is better described as *subjectivist*. This is not simply a matter of terminology because the fact that relativism is characterised in subjectivist terms means that the debate is polarised between the relativism of individual taste or opinion, on the one hand, and the morality of absolutes, on the other. The familiar crusading tone is then adopted.

It *is* a matter of objective truth whether a particular group of people hold certain values. What this does not show is whether these values are right or wrong. We certainly need more than this. It is perhaps true, as SCAA claim, that once the possibility of objective moral truth is denied, much academic and other endeavour becomes pointless (SCAA, 1996, p.10). Objectivity is, of course, compatible with relativism – in matters of etiquette, for instance, as we shall see. But this is not the kind of objectivity that is being claimed for morality. For all the variations in belief and value that do exist between individuals and groups, there are, it is claimed, *universal* moral truths. (In etiquette, it seems clear, there are none.)

It is worth asking what other kinds of universal truth there are in order to see what this implies about morality. Perhaps the best example of universality in familiar curriculum terms is to be found in mathematics. Seven times five is thirty-five (provided we are working in base 10) is true now, always, everywhere, and for everybody. In fact, this last phrase scarcely makes sense as, once you have understood the sum, you cannot really imagine what it could mean for it not to be true. There is something timeless about such truths, then, and they seem not to be relative to context at all. These are the kinds of things we have to accept, uncritically, if we are to bring critical understanding to bear on particular problems – in fact, if we are going to do maths at all.

Puzzles remain nevertheless. Are these truths 'already there' – that is, were they so before there were any human beings to put them into words? Or are they the products of human endeavour – in fact, spectacular cultural achievements developed over several thousand years? If it is right to speak of *discovering* the truth, it seems at least that they must be something beyond purely human products. One thing that is noticeable with maths – not so much with elementary sums like the one above but more especially with difficult calculations that we struggle with – is that when we come to see the correct answer it is as though the truth forces itself on us: we cannot but see that this is the case. Mathematical proof works like this. Perhaps in science things are not quite so clear but it is central to science that evidence from experiment is compelling. (You cannot *not* accept the evidence, unless you can show something unsound about it.) This is quite unlike those circumstances in our lives where we have a measure of choice. In a sense, in maths and science at least, we step out of our individual viewpoints to join a universal way of seeing things. We are not dealing with matters of opinion. Of course, similar arguments can be advanced in the case of other subjects but it is worth keeping maths in mind as a kind of gold standard for what can count as objective and universal truth. Maths seems to provide the best case for the claims of absolutism.

Given the crude absolutism of Mrs Jimmon, presumably the 'truths' by which she lives her life are as plain and unassailable to her, as written-into-the-universe, as that two plus two is four. But morality does not have to be like this. In fact, it cannot really be like this, as her fate in the story seems to show. It is plain that the SCAA position, the position amplified by

Marianne Talbot and Nick Tate, is more carefully qualified than this but the linking of objectivity to absolutism is maintained. How far is this right?

In the case of etiquette it is objectively true not only that people in a particular community *believe* that you should, say, eat with your fork in your left hand but that in that community this is *truly* what you should do. In other words, what is right in such matters is determined by local practice. (When in Rome, do as the Romans do.) You watch people playing a game you don't know. To join in you have to go along with what they do. Join a community, belong to a community, and it is rather as if you have to obey the rules of their game. In a similar way, what is correct in a language is determined by what people do and not by some standard beyond this. This is a matter of objectivity, though not of universal absolutes.

How do we learn what is right and wrong in these practices? From our infancy we are reared into diverse practices that form the background conditions of meaning to what we go on to do; and throughout life we take up, or are taken up into, new practices in this way. We must come to do what others do. Clearly this is not a matter of personal judgement or taste. And if that sounds hopelessly conformist, it is worth remembering two things: first, we scarcely become social beings, which is to say that we can scarcely become people, unless we take on the practices of our communities in this way; and second, this still leaves plenty of scope for doing our own thing. In fact, we can only be autonomous against such a background of taken-for-granted practices and beliefs, just as a footballer can only play creatively if it is already taken for granted what football is all about.

Now there is some reason to believe that morality involves something more than this – something more than these conventions, so they seem – and that the idea that there are absolutes here has rather more going for it. It was said that in maths the truth forces itself on you. In language learning or in matters of etiquette this is not the case, although, of course, some practices will come to be recognised as indubitably correct. But correctness here is just a matter of the done thing: in moral matters what is right sometimes strikes us with a force of a different order than our sense of propriety in these other cases. (Part of Mrs Jimmon's problem is her crass insensitivity to the contours of obligation.) Truth sometimes forces itself on us in matters of morality, but it does this not in abstract principles or general propositions but in the concrete reality of the particular case. You are sitting watching television and the door-bell rings. You go to answer and find no-one there but a baby in a cardboard box. *Of course* you should help the baby abandoned on your door-step. Does anybody seriously doubt this? The baby places an absolute demand on you in this particular case and given these circumstances. If you have to think this through, you have already failed to respond to the nature of the moral demand. Why imagine next that there is some over-arching principle in accordance with which you must act? How does seeing it in this way help, or make you any more moral? Such a calculation of principle – certain kinds of utilitarianism, say – might be the very thing that blinds you to the immediate ethical demands on your doorstep.

In cases like this there is scarcely any role for 'searching for the truth about moral matters' – you would have to be morally blind not to see this. In the daily run of our lives perhaps we should be grateful that the moral issues that confront us are not so extreme or clear. In our daily lives then we must search for the right thing to do. What will be needed in our search is greater sensitivity to the particular case, not the universal rules of moral absolutism. We will need to be able to see things from different points of view and under different descriptions so that our response is not deadened by a dominant tranquillised understanding of the world. The kinds of guidance that abstract moral principles provide can stand in the way here, encouraging instead complacency and hubris.

If this is right, better analogies for morality amongst curriculum subjects will be found in the arts, those subjects where objectivity involves attention to the particulars we are dealing with – to painting, music, texts. And this last is especially significant in view of the ways that reading relates so closely to, and can enhance, the moral life. Consider the words of A. S. Byatt comparing her own formative reading – her moral education – with that of her niece:

> One of my greatest moments of moral recognition was when I read about Emma being rude to Miss Bates and realising that she had done something unpardonable and had hurt somebody. This struck at my soul and I have never been the same since. My niece read half of *Emma* on her summer holiday and then came home. She began again her normal practice of watching *Neighbours* and telephoning her friends

and talking to them for two hours about what the people in *Neighbours* ought to have done. You can argue that this is exactly the same sort of moral discovery as my discovery that Emma had done something terrible, but I don't believe it is because it was missing the kind of relationship between the seriousness of Jane Austen placing that for all of us and the seriousness of me alone, taking that in. I think that my niece needs both; she needs *Emma* and she needs to talk like crazy to her friends about what the characters from *Neighbours* should have done. (Van Reid, 1992, p. 17)

Watching *Neighbours* and reading Jane Austen will each help to reveal contours of the moral landscape but the 'seriousness' of Jane Austen will register fine gradations and extremes which otherwise escape the attention. There is something important here about the *quality* of our imagination and its relation to our perception of the situations in which we find ourselves, where imagination is not something fanciful and superfluous but is unavoidable ('the seriousness of ... taking that in'). But it is difficult to attend to the contextual nature of our moral lives in this way when the demand is for absolutes.

If absolutism is essential to morality, this reveals a further problem. Mrs Jimmon's absolute morality is, of course, of the most synthetic kind. There are fundamentalist religions, in contrast, where the letter of the law of a robust morality is derived unswervingly from the letter of the book. Don't these religions have exemplary absolutist credentials? In fact, their precision and certainty make SCAA look tentative. We might pause to be grateful for the fact that the recommendations we have are qualified in this way – evidence, presumably, of the diversity of views represented at the conference. Of course, fundamentalists disagree more vehemently than anyone else and we can only guess at how SCAA would have progressed if it had been made up only of them. But disagreement is surely not the issue here: if truth is absolute it certainly does not depend on the beliefs people happen to hold or on how many of them agree! (They might think differently, putting us back in the quagmire of relativism.) So there is something of a puzzle when lists of absolutes are presented as a *result* of their work. Comparison is made to the ease with which the business world arrives at its mission statements, but these are not presumably absolute in the way that moral truths are claimed to be. There is a problem then about what SCAA is doing in getting people together to arrive at lists of moral absolutes. If it is objected that the purpose is not to determine the source of values but rather to find areas of agreement, this may well be justified as a pragmatic and prudent measure. But it should be recognised that this seriously undermines the *authority* that these values have. Given an absolutist framework, the sources are the reasons for accepting the values. Conceding the legitimacy of disagreement over sources is tantamount to conceding relativism. (It is the sources that make the values real.) SCAA is caught unsteadily between moral absolutism and a prevailing liberal democratic concern with consensus and social harmony. Its procedures tend to smooth over differences: it is true that dissent is acknowledged in the documents, but in such a way as to contain it.

At a time when few people involved with education can say very much at all without reference to efficiency and effectiveness, it should cause no great surprise that instrumentalism creeps in here: 'an effective and just society is based on the assumption that certain rules are acceptable to a wide range of individuals' (SCAA, 1995, p. 6). Yes, we want a just society, but an *effective* one? Effective for what? Effectiveness has its sense in the light of particular ends. If these are unspecified it leaves open a variety of possibilities, and what will be effective will be relative to those ends. Bland consensus over absolutes dulls the sense that these are live questions. It shifts debate from ends to means, and so gives away democracy to the instrumentalism of the age. Agreement over not very much suppresses larger visions of the good, of the good society and of the good life. New Labour's commitment to promoting social inclusion will cease to be genuinely pluralistic if it slides into this kind of hollow conformism.

If educators today can say little without deferring to effectiveness, neither can they say much without some genuflection towards individual choice. Individuals must, it seems, develop their own value system: 'Society permits, even if it does not promote, a range of behaviour which is considered wrong by some, often many, of its members ... The task of schools, in partnership with the home, is to furnish pupils with the knowledge and the ability to question and reason which will enable them to develop their own value system and to make responsible decisions on such matters' (*ibid.*, pp. 5-6). But doesn't the vocabulary of an *individual value system* re-construct morality as a matter of individual preference (and so re-introduce the relativism that was under attack)? If not, what is it that is being developed? Of course morality involves choice but this way of speaking tunes in with the idea that our values are things that we choose. Rather they are things that impress themselves on us – the basis on which we choose. Think of values as the result of choice and society is itself instrumentalised to the satisfaction of its individual members or, worse, to some economic measure.

We have seen that the polarisation of the discussion between moral absolutism, on the one hand, and a subjectivist conception of relativism, on the other, is apt to screen out the importance of community. Something of this seems to be captured in parts of the short chapter on morality in Melanie Phillips' *All Must Have Prizes*. She begins:

> The extreme, value-neutral doctrines handed down to the schools in Britain and America were an expression of a profound cultural shift in which to be judgmental was to be accused of attempting to limit the perfect entitlement of individuals to make up the rules for themselves. It was the apotheosis of individualism, and it had become the defining value of the culture. And since education is the process by which a society hands down the values of its culture from one generation to the next, that was now being handed down. Individualism was indeed the one thing that could be handed down in a culture which no longer believed in the validity of handing down any kind of tradition. Paradoxically, the only certainty that could be allowed was that there were no certainties, and the only judgment was that there must be no judgements. The individual self was the summation of all that was true and valuable, choice was sacrosanct and rights trumped all. The concept of a common culture, common bonds and a shared story that we needed to tell each other in order to survive as a common enterprise became synonymous with oppression. The individual stood entirely alone. The 'me society' became synonymous with democracy and freedom itself. (Phillips, 1996, p. 219)

The emphasis is echoed at the end of the chapter in remarks from Jonathan Sacks which she quotes at the end of the chapter. Sacks suggests that moralities, like languages, involve a paradox: 'only by yielding to something that is not individual can we become individuals'; only by 'apprenticeship in the rules and virtues of a moral tradition can we shape the life that we alone are called on to live. Like languages, moralities are not universal' (*ibid.*, p. 231). We can no more sustain relationships without rules than we can communicate without rules of grammar. We need then a common tradition, a common culture, a shared story. Although we are moving in a helpful direction, however, Phillips' gloss on this points towards the universal in a way that is at odds with what is otherwise being said here. She reaches beyond to 'moral principles that are common to us all' (*ibid.*, p. 232).

There are other ways in which her position is unclear, as is seen in her response to remarks of Graham Haydon. Haydon considers the pupil who asks 'How do we know that this is right and that is wrong?' It is not acceptable, he suggests, to respond by saying either 'Because I say so' or 'because these are the values of your society'. But for Phillips this stance on the part of the teacher is typical of that reluctance to impose values that is a part of relativism. Now this is a bit odd given the fact that Haydon's point of view derives very much from the tradition of liberal education (with the questioning Socrates in the background) which in other respects Phillips seems eager to embrace. Is this the relativism that must be so roundly condemned? There may be some point in attacking these ways of thought but one should bear in mind that in so doing one undermines faith in universal reason, as Nigel Blake's chapter in this volume makes clear. Haydon's purpose is hardly to endorse the idea that we cannot know what is right and wrong. It is to favour reason-giving over blind acceptance of authority. The greater the faith in universal reason the more legitimate this question becomes.

Phillips' response to the pupil is: 'Because these are the values of our common humanity and are the basis of human flourishing.' On the one hand, this seems to imply (correctly) that there is so much that we must accept before we can ask meaningful questions; as with learning a language, we must begin by adopting or copying the practices of our community. On the other, it asks us to move to a different plane as if the moral life must be underwritten by something that is abstract and universal.

It is worth considering the kind of effect a remark like this is likely to have. What job is the statement of principle doing? It is the kind of remark that moves someone who is already won over, a kind of reassurance for the converted. To someone who is not, it may be alienating, adding another layer, and an abstract one at that, to the peculiar institution of morality (see John White's chapter in this volume). For many the very word 'morality' has become tainted, suggesting the stiff correctness of Victorian behaviour, sexual repression (if not hang-ups), timid subjection to conformity, and a certain starchiness of tone. And there is a danger of the whole idea being reduced – to the 'common sense' of the Moral Majority or to a whole package of right-on non-judgmental political correctness. People *do* avoid speaking of morality – as if something were amiss with it, as with an outmoded ceremony. Are we using a language whose significance for us has faded from view – not so much the problem SCAA identifies of confusion arising from varying interpretations of key terms but a deeper problem of the dislocation of a whole way of speaking, a way for us to understand, and live with, ourselves and our world? Words come to seem like shadows of a way of relating to one another that no longer quite gains purchase on our lives or quite makes sense. Remarks about people's common humanity, or even about human flourishing, can sound lofty and rhetorical, interrupting the flow of people's ordinary (morally charged) engagement with the world. If there is a problem of dislocation, it is hardly put right by an appeal to the universal. Indeed that may be the source of the trouble. Remarks like these take away the rich contextualisation that gives the sense of right and wrong its force.

In speaking of 'our common humanity' Phillips adopts phrasing similar to those remarks of Marianne Talbot and Nick Tate in Chapter 1 that we must instil '*our* values, the values to which every person of goodwill would subscribe'. But – an obvious point – who does this 'our' refer to? To use the word is to assume in advance that there are those common features that the arguments claim to demonstrate. Given a universal sense ('our common humanity') the appeal seems to be to some kind of constant human nature: *we* are to be contrasted with Martians and with mice.

The more this universality, this common human nature, is emphasised, the more precarious become claims about culture. Culture and morality are internally related – you cannot have one without the other. To speak of a culture or tradition that we share makes most sense when *our* culture is contrasted with *theirs*, and this must mean other people's and not the 'culture' of mice or Martians. Cultures and traditions relate to particular peoples, places, and products. Some moral values can no longer apply as the conditions in which they made sense no longer exist. (Take the codes of honour and chivalry for the medieval knight.) Some change with context, perhaps out of all recognition. (What counts as courage.) They can evaporate when they are encompassed by assumptions of universality, and this seems to be recognised in Sacks' remarks. We no more learn a universal morality than a universal language because neither exists. There is an unresolved tension in Phillips' ideas between the authority of culture and tradition and a commitment to absolutism and to a universal reason. Of course, there are overlaps between the moralities of different cultures and, of course, on countless occasions there is no problem in seeing what is right and what is wrong. Neither should there necessarily be any problem in standing up for what is right. But the rightness and wrongness emerge in particular locations and contexts and they are right or wrong because of those contexts, not because of some universal ingredient. To imagine a universal ingredient is to construct a superstratum that diverts us from proper attention to the messy stuff of our ordinary moral lives.

We can avoid further confusion if we remember that no-one in their right mind seriously asks whether mugging old ladies or cruelty to cats are right. The wrongness is built into the descriptions, just as evil is by definition wrong – so there can be no question of respecting someone's views that this is not the case (SCAA, 1996, p. 8). Is this something we need to be taught? Do you teach children that murder is wrong? The wrongness is built into our world and the young child absorbs this as part of the background. If she does not or if she wants to do (this kind of) wrong, it is not that she doesn't know the rules: something has gone wrong with her world.

One lesson that the story of Mr Jimmon and his family provides is that there are situations in life where reliance on rules lets us down. Now much of our lives is governed by rules and it is clear that schools have multiple rules, whether these are spelled out or not. Obeying them, or not obeying them, can become preoccupations for pupils, and a preoccupation for some teachers as well. But there are different types of rule and differences in the way these are learned. Some rules, the most obvious perhaps, regulate behaviour and these can easily be made explicit: don't do this, do do that. But there are constitutive rules which go to make up the activities we engage in: the grammar of a language is a case in point. In fact all social practices incorporate constitutive rules: we could not be people without them.

We might arrive at some common ground by agreeing some minimal sets of regulative rules but in terms of constitutive rules this scarcely makes sense. Such a negotiated settlement might work as a kind of stand-off or way of getting along for people with conflicting views, absolutist or otherwise. This would not reveal any universal morality but would be a means for peaceful coexistence and for sustaining the rhythms of communal life. But to imagine that morality is centrally a matter of regulative rules gets the whole landscape wrong. The regulative comes to usurp the place of meaning in our moral geography, covering it over with abstract grid lines of control. In fact, clear rules cover over the difficulty that *responsibility* to our circumstances must face. The regulative can seduce us with its formal appeal, seeming to dissolve the messy complexities of our ordinary experience.

This is the appeal of systematic moralism. It can erode the presupposition of trust that is fundamental to the circumstances in which those constitutive rules are passed on – circumstances where we are from the start confronted by others, by people who look after us but also look to us in anticipation. From our beginnings, we discover ourselves in the faces of others as they respond to us, and in the response they look for in return. This expectation of response from us is there from our earliest awakenings. It casts us as responsible from the start. We are responsible before we are anything else. For all the current talk of 'responsibility', it is as if modern usage has quite obscured the breadth of significance of this answering to others.

It is then at the level of neither the universal nor the subjective that morality must be located but at the intermediate level of the communal with its presupposition of trust and of the regard of others. It is these communal bonds that are essential to morality and to the development of anything like citizenship. And on this view it doesn't seem likely that a new concern with 'social capital' or with the 'stake-holder' society will get things quite right, seeming, as they respectively do, to import notions of the market and of the social contract. It is not such a great exaggeration to say that morality is everything or it is nothing. Communal bonds must extend beyond the family and the familiar to incorporate something of the unknown. The family exists in order ultimately to fragment. This darker side to the family relates to a tension between our loyalties to those we are closest to and our duty to those within a larger ambit. The deeper point behind the shadow of incest is that over-concern with self-sufficiency and with preserving one's own kind threatens the life of the community and jeopardises morality. Mr Jimmon's disturbing pragmatism combines with his deepest commitment: his responsibilities as a husband and father are funnelled into a preserving of his own kind. Virtuous family love refracts into vice. Living within the narrowest circle of intimacy can mean exclusion from *any* community.

If we cannot get far without communal bonds, what kind of authority do they imply? A kind of authoritarianism *is* involved, especially when it comes to the upbringing of young children. As we have seen, they do not simply emerge as autonomous beings who judge whether or not they should obey rules. Rather they reach autonomy after a process of acculturation. What does this amount to? It may be objected that this is a kind of indoctrination, but this is hardly the case as what is passed on is scarcely doctrine. Rather it is a matter of 'what we do'. It is an open question how far this acculturation must extend through a person's life, and in what ways and to what extent autonomy must develop, but it seems likely that in some degree it never ends. That there must be this acculturation, that the learner must accept up to a point that this is what is done, is beyond doubt. Without this the learner can scarcely be a person. This is the latent truth in Phillips' account, one that is suppressed by the preoccupations she shares with Tate about the dangers of relativism.

Preoccupation with regulative rules smacks of a loss of faith in – and fast becomes a loss of commitment to – those moral bonds that make up our communities. I have argued that moral absolutism desensitises us to context and reduces responsibility. The louder the appeals to common-sense universal truths, the more threadbare the fabric of our moral lives is seen to be. Just as culture can evaporate, so these necessary communities can disappear at the behest of ghostly movements of market forces.

What needs to be recovered is the middle ground of morality, the only ground on which we can live. And this is not some compromise between the absolute and the subjective. The absolute is a metaphysical chimera; the subjective can only emerge out of a communal space in which not just morality but meaning itself is given to our lives, the space in which our lives take their shape. Fiction often captures this better than abstract theory and more faithfully than the media-influenced terms of the current debate. People may be sceptical about speaking of 'morality'. But witness the strong reactions and responses to events in *Brookside*. In fact we live our lives in and through the kinds of stories that are available to us, and while these can enlighten they can also brutalise and desensitise: morality is not the mantra of rules that Mrs Jimmon lives by, tranquillised as she is by the fiction of Los Angeles.

The voice of plain speaking surreptitiously revives memories of a fabled world of absolutes with its characteristically English heroics and its dragon to be slain. Its bold assertions of common sense can intimidate, closing off possibilities of more considered response and polarising debate. It makes more plausible the idea of absolutes and of a simpler fabulous world of right and wrong. But it does this at the expense of morality and education.

Notes

1. Quotations from Nick Tate throughout this chapter are, unless otherwise stated, from his address to this conference, as reported by Nicholas Pyke in the *Times Educational Supplement* on 19 January 1996.

2. In the destruction by fire and brimstone of the iniquitous city of Sodom, Lot and his wife and daughters are spared. They are told to flee to the mountains and not to look back. His wife looks back and is turned into a pillar of salt. His daughters make him drink wine and then sleep with him in his oblivion. Both bear sons who in turn father the Moabites and the Ammonites. (*Genesis*, 19)

Chapter 5

The Spirit of Moral Education – or what, subject to my will, you will

Tony Skillen

We get morally educated and miseducated by life. We push someone aside and are sworn at. We ignore an 'unimportant' acquaintance and only later come to see that we have thereby wronged them. Or we fail to go to someone's help, passing by on the other side, and only on reflection realise the twist in priorities that left us unmoved. With great acuteness and passion, we talk about our intimates, friends and acquaintances; about them and their unfairnesses, snobberies or meannesses; about their untrust-worthiness, spinelessness, tyranny or cruelty. In flash-floods, steady streams or obscure leaks, the position is painfully reversed, and we find ourselves on the low moral ground, a lesson, with luck, in objectivity and humility. We appreciate and admire people for what they do, and also for their responses, their way of taking things. We are not very old before we have a nose for hypocrisy, inconsistency, and posing in all manner of moral fancy-dress. We soon learn and need to deceive ourselves to maintain a sense of dignity when we give off such odours – tacitly inverted testimony to straightforwardness and integrity. The 'we' in all this is the generality of persons, whether members of Neighbourhood Watch or a street gang; it is not restricted to the bourgeois goody-goody or the holier-than-them. Any conception of moral education as pumping air in to an otherwise uninflated ball – that, in matters of morality, nature supplies only a vacuum – is false to the everyday moral density, sophistication, suppleness and subtlety of even the crudest and narrowest thought, feeling, discourse and activity.

From infancy we are ethically responsive beings. Members of our species are programmed to respond differentially to love and hostility, to warmth and neglect, to fidelity and betrayal. We do not merely learn from experience, we bring to our developing experiences a developing moral perspective, such that our lives are, from the start, infused by expectations of each other which are not just statistical predictions but holdings-to-account: so that we do not merely feel fear or frustration, pleasure or relief, but suspicion and anger, love and appreciation. We are from an early age capable not only of being disappointed by people but disappointed in them. The experiences we learn from, then, are already morally inflected. And so, as we grow into the world, we come to have a not altogether coherent and largely tacit awareness of ourselves and of those around us as human beings, valued or devalued, loved or rejected. That these moral capacities and dispositions struggle against others in our spiritual ecosystem, that they might be drowned out by greed or vanity, is not because, unlike greed or vanity, they are not natural and need to be instilled. Greed and vanity, natural as they are, have their own social sourcing and stimuli and are daily instilled by inducement, example and flattery – you get a star at school for your classroom considerateness: what does that teach you, exactly? And, given the differentials in power between children and adults, it is as 'natural' for a child to come to think ill of himself or herself, to devalue themselves or to think themselves no good, as to think and feel the opposite. Indeed, not only is it possible for someone simultaneously to act as if they were the centre of the world and to think themselves worthless, the former may in part be a consequence of the latter. You have been the target of malign neglect since you can remember – what does that tell you about yourself, roughly?

There is an unintended conspiracy among intellectuals and public moralists to lose the sense of the banal treasure of our more or less consensual moral vocabulary. Philosophers, for example, commonly make their trade out of the erection and demolition of Universal Principles. Their classical focus in research and teaching is on counter-examples to such Principles or on dilemmas which expose their fragility. The hidden 'moral' of all this conjecture and refutation is that the discussible complexity of concrete moral life is somehow an embarrassment to the idea of objective thinking in such matters. And so you get students, who, having over their morning tea been berating some treacherous partner or thoughtless roommate, come into their seminar and solemnly aver the pure privacy, relativity, subjectivity or whatever, of 'morality'. ('Next week we will discuss abortion.') With a vested interest in theory, abstraction and terms whose meanings we lay down, we professionals have been encouraging each other and our students to think of the thick undergrowth of moral sensibility as an absence of cleared and signposted pathways. Yet the students' 'gossip' has been subtle in itself – 'It's not that he minds clearing up; he just seems to assume a good fairy will do it for him' – and also it has presupposed a familiarity with context and individuals that has already taken it beyond the scope of the classroom 'example'. Hence these extra-curricular Solomons metamorphose into Foolish Virgins or Clever Lawyers taking up positions for tutelary purposes.

Meanwhile, the headline sense of Morality continues to be as limited as ever to the domains of sex and shoplifting – *Vicar's Lover Nicks Nightie* – with a quite callous disregard for the complexity of sexual life or for the degree of restraint and prudence required and shown nowadays in negotiating the temptations of an unsupervised party or supermarket. If 'Moral' is so frequently coupled with 'Crisis', 'Breakdown', 'Debate' and now 'Maze', it is no wonder we get into a panic when we have to put on our best suit and think explicitly about moral life. It is as if, in matters aesthetic, we forgot about parks, gardens and kicked-over litter-bins in wondering over the question whether we have any common sense of Beauty and Ugliness. Moral situations are often clear, but they are not thereby lacking in complexity: we are born with the capacity to handle complexity. Our moral intuitions in the rough-and-tumble of everyday experience are often more reasonable than the reasons we verbalise in their support or defence, which is not to say that reflection may not properly lead to their revision. Anyone knows this, and novelists and dramatists depend on it for their livelihood. So it is a strange fact that the mind goes on a sort of earnest holiday when it is asked to think about 'matters of morality', as serious a thing as we could ask it to think about.

On the basis of his observations of children's play and talk, the Swiss psychologist Jean Piaget argued that there was a spontaneous progress in the child's moral understanding. Piaget's notion of genetically fixed 'stages' has been rightly questioned. He seems to have underestimated children, partly through too much reliance on explicit interviews rather than on observation and listening. But Piaget thought that the main thing revealed by his researches was the fact of an inherent capacity for moral development that arose and expressed itself in the guts of children's interactions in parks and playgrounds outside the supervision and surveillance of parents and teachers. The sense of rules, fairness, generosity and sensitivity to particular needs and capacities shown by children playing marbles belied what he thought of as the external and authoritarian model of moral upbringing. On that model, through imposition by adult authorities, morality gets 'internalised' in the child who, so to speak, becomes his own policeman, governing himself. This process is sometimes thought of in terms of the behavioural replacement of autistic childish impulse by mature habit, sometimes as occurring through the child's coming to identify him or herself with authority-figures at home or school. In some views, this internalisation requires the child to form a conception of an ultimate lawgiver and omniscient judge and sanctioner: God. Piaget's children got on with their marbles in the absence of such higher powers. But the authoritarian model is of rules descending to control and channel little boys who would otherwise be scrapping and trying to kill each other with stones, transforming this natural mayhem into a regulated and proper procedure. In some hands the model has been of Civilisation pitted against Savagery; in others of Humanity against the Beast in Us; in yet others of Spirit's war with Flesh or the Superego's assault on the Id. In any case, it is monitoring, conquering, taming, subjugating and punishing that is envisaged as the main mode of moralisation, until a Second Nature predominates over its primal predecessor – '... children need to be introduced from an early age to the concepts of right and wrong so that moral behaviour becomes an instinctive habit.'

The institution of the 'schoolchild' is the embodiment of this image of protracted metamorphosis. Universal schooling was in many ways a social mechanism for the control of boys and girls otherwise hell-bent for an urchin life on the streets or in competition with their elders for employment. John Locke, the Father of the Liberal Enlightenment, thought school no place for a young gentleman – his writing on education, like that of Rousseau in the next century, is largely a rule-book for personal tutoring and practical experience. But he did advocate the setting up of schools for the 'labouring poor's' offspring, who, whether wandering the streets neglected or depriving their mothers of the liberty to earn a wage, were 'an ordinary burden to the parish':

The most effectual remedy for this and which we therefore humbly propose is that ... working schools be set up in every parish, to which the children of all such as demand relief from the parish, above three and under fourteen years of age, whilst they live at home with their parents and are not otherwise employed for their livelihood by the allowance of the overseers of the poor, shall be obliged to come.

At this place, the children's schoolwork was to consist of 'spinning and knitting', save on Sundays when they would attend only so as 'to be brought into some sense of religion'. Thus, adequately fed, the children would be 'inured to work', 'made sober and industrious all their lives after' and be a 'minimal burden to parents and parish', rather than the strangers equally to work, religion and morality that Locke found them to be.

The German philosopher Kant, a century later, took a more positive view of the benefits of tutelary congregation than did Locke. Although their curriculum was to be one of mental labour, and their goal the formation of a Rational Individual, he shared the laborious view of schools' processing with his English predecessor:

> It is discipline which prevents man from being turned aside by his animal impulses from humanity, his appointed end ... By discipline, men are placed in subjection to the laws of mankind and brought to feel their constraint. Children, for instance, are first sent to school, not so much with the object of their learning something but rather that they may become used to sitting still and doing exactly as they are told ... The love of freedom is naturally so strong in man that, when once he has grown accustomed to freedom, he will sacrifice everything for its sake. For this reason, discipline must be brought into play very early; for when this has not been done, it is difficult to alter character later in life ... We see this among savage nations who have never become accustomed to European manners.

Poorhouse-like, monastery-like, prison-like, factory-like, asylum-like, the modern school's structures and routines have their strange but still visible archaeology. This is a better explanation of the failure of twentieth-century progressivism than its supposed optimism about the spontaneous capacities of young human beings to discover, co-operate and mature morally. For all their big windows (something else not to break, something else not to stare at), the modern Plowdenised schools still had the same premises; it was largely a matter of greater freedoms of association within the constrictions of those premisses and of the attempt to develop class-management strategies that could turn a group of thirty into a community of mutually affirming and disciplining individuals. Tasks beyond the reach of a brilliant and charismatic saint, let alone a modern hit-squad, were charged to members of a profession of moderate social standing, entry to which has largely not been sought by those with the 'ability' and 'ambition' and 'qualifications' to 'do something better with themselves'. Except insofar as it took the brutal edge off classroom practice, progressivism failed. Sometimes it became the mask of inattentive and acquiescent teaching. But beware of those who hanker after the white-knuckle terror and tedium of the average good-old day! As if the two hundred years before Plowden and the post-war changes had been a paradise of pious performance, the modernised regimentalists are back with a National Curriculum of dumbing narrowness and a spirit-at-large of surveillance and audit, of defensive preparation for tests and inspections, of the sacrifice of the necessary intimacies and spontaneities of the teaching relationship to the gridlocked requirements of accountancy, including moral accountancy.

Bringing in business people to reinforce the putative connection between educability today and employability tomorrow, they undertake the 'contracting' parents to reinforce the idea that being tough on failure entails also arraigning the supposed causes of failure. And, though the Laws of Supply and Demand have yet to be modified for this purpose, bad teachers are to be replaced from a stock of good teachers set aside for the purpose. Are these to be flockless priests or redundant middle-managers? One sees no queue of young men and women eager to enter the realm of public servitude under the going conditions. Meanwhile, such is the status accorded this vocation, that the idea that educators should themselves have an education is being replaced with the idea that all they need instead is on-the-job training. How, not being expected to have it themselves, are teachers supposed to be in the hunt to communicate any loving grasp of any subject to those under their management?

The most morally loaded part of the schoolchild's day is that spent, now under low-waged under-supervision, in the playground. It is there that likes and dislikes, affiliations and fissions, games and fights, conversations and rows, affirmations and mockery, status-seeking and simplicity, warmth and bullying, sharing and hogging – the textural detail of ordinary moral life – are stoked-up or reined-in and given their local stamp. It is there that the politics of passion and judgement thrive, not in a bipolar relation of subject-to-authority but in one of multifocal contest and co-operation among peers. For all the Mission Statements of school ethos, for all the Statements of Values, with their requisite communitarian rhetoric about children 'living together', 'sharing, helping and caring for each other', the class and corridor life of the official school world is an ethically thinned-out one, deliberately stripped down in such a way as to foreground the narrow and negative ideals of submission, tidiness, quiet, order, keeping 'hands, feet and objects to ourselves' and not interfering with or stealing from each other. Within this cleared arena, it is a matter of individuals knuckling 'autonomously' down to work, moralised as not letting yourself or your parents down or preventing 'neighbours' and 'chums' from succeeding (in the 'real' world represented by the man in the grey flannel suit addressing the Assembly about the ethical dimension of company service).

Centuries of fables, parables, sermons, commandments and statements of universal principles or 'value systems' are pressed into the service of these drably codable functions. But these anthems help to confuse the taken-for-granted peculiarities of the school arena with the general predicaments of life. After all, any environment implies its own characteristic temptations and deviant rewards; and nobody is going to advocate the virtues of damage or disruption. Even in a prison camp, the individual rebel, whatever his or her motives, is liable to incur not only suffering and disadvantage, but to make things worse for everybody. By any criterion, this consequence is not a Good Thing. But these truisms are not an argument for that environment, its structure or functions. Generally, these structures, considered as a child's daily world, are as mean as the streets from which they are designed to keep him. And generally, these functions are as base as the rapacious world within which the school's products are expected, whether obediently or enterprisingly, to compete for survival. Locke and Kant wanted to form competent-enough and pious-enough personalities, inured to labour and obedient to duty; the new technology only changes the skills demanded by the tigers of the lambs. Yet, somehow, this world, too mean to commit resources to the new generation's nurture, is to harvest the profit of this self-denying preparatory process, in the form of a more moral citizen and a more tractable subject. You can be sure that something is amiss in the meaning of the word 'culture' when people reach for the gun of moralism to clean it up. Why is it that morality's official spokespersons become so activated in times of deep 'constraints' on the public purse?

The regimentalists have never been completely blind to the contextual obstacles to their vision of behavioral virtue. Thus, while appealing for philanthropic support from any particular millionaire, they lament the general materialism of the age; while striving officiously to prepare their charges to survive in the hard and demanding world of business, they condemn the 'consumer' values which are essential to business. ('We are pleased, boys and girls, to have with us to-day the UK Community Service Officer from Nike, who will put to us all the challenging question: Are You a Loser?'); while condemning 'moral relativism', they strive to attach their target-audience to one or other of the established religions, denominations or sects colluding and competing for their allegiance. While claiming to promote 'critical understanding', they promulgate notions of deference to national, religious and 'community' leaders, and the swallowing of their self-uplifting historical myths; while claiming to uphold family values, they teach children that their errant parents must be contractually subjected to the school authorities' demands; while panicking about the corruptions of the youth-media and the 'synthetic world' of youth culture, they drive their Pinocchios into the relieving embrace of hosts that appear more responsive to young people's preoccupations and wit than the increasingly cold-faced school. These contextual thrusts and shuffles involve a functional self-deception about the real world's powers and the real potentialities of the child. At least the élite in pre-democratic times was more honest within itself about 'School and Society'.

'Care in the Community' is a value almost destroyed by the budgetary motivations masked by its anti-authoritarian and communitarian rhetoric. So, any movement towards 'deschooling' the lives of young people would create chaos in the absence of a practical recognition of the dovetailing of schooling into the whole fabric of our lives. For this reason, some who strive to connect children with the wider society offer consumer-adjusted programmes of work-experience and community service limited to sundry 'partnerships' with existing local authority or business establishments, while others contemplate teacher-controlled community service initiatives. Others still have Princely notions of selected volunteers earning career-points by engaging in more ambitious projects. In every case, the community-cadets are envisaged as docile do-gooders or trainees, while, yet again the supply of adult supervisory inputs is dreamt-up as coming from men of goodwill, churches and mosques, and suitably incentivised agencies. Instead of a paradigm-shift in our notion of young people in society, a notion that would correlatively implicate our notion of old people in society, what we have is a paradigm-juggle, in effect a return to conceptions of the Scouts and the Boys' Brigade, if not to the old work-house. This is not, to put it as succinctly as possible within the space allocated, on.

Children are not stupid; or rather, they are no more stupid, and often more alert, than their elders. They pick up, with normal precocity, the nature of the world around, behind and ahead of them. Nor are they congenitally lazier or significantly more selfish than their life-models. They learn, with all its built-in creative refractoriness, the child role. There are structural limits on the sorts of role that can be learned and taught in a world dominated by the imperatives of capitalist regulation, with its inherent potential, in pursuit of the cheapest and most trainable sector of humanity, to pressgang the young into its immediate service. But the Wilberforcean ideology of child-protection has functioned as a debilitating buffer between the child and what he or she is to mature into. The hypothesis that capital can be tamed and its rapacity sublimated is an article of faith for any civilised contemporary regime. But when it comes to education, the assumption is that it is the young who must be protected and tamed – domesticated, in order that the global market will eventually grace them with employment. We are even deafer to the seriousness of children than we are to their playfulness. We rob them of a life of growing participation and contribution as well as of the companionship and advice of their elders of all ages. We abstract them from the richly educative world of things and people, stories and theories, and expect them to swot it all up in some York Notes version. No wonder even those who get to University arrive there with the reflexes of battery chickens released onto the grass. Genuine Care in the Community for people of all ages involves us all in a lifelong-learning experience which respects our differences without erecting dichotomous worlds, and which respects our commonality without all-day penning. Given the perennial flop that is School's blitz on the Three Rs, is it not surprising that there is not an inquiry among our Educational Dignitaries into the proposition that these necessities might be better and more rapidly learned in an environment which differs from the one that so illusorily seemed immaculately conceived for their inculcation? Must these fanatics redouble their efforts by halving the time spent on art, music and theatre? And similarly, given the moral flop of school life, is it not surprising that the proponents of the Moral Nomenclatura do not, instead of amplifying the sermons, contemplate amplifying the scope of young people's human experience? Must the halls be made even more giggle-threateningly silent that our children may learn to behave in happy fellowship?

As Aristotle said, you learn ethically by doing. He was concerned mainly with the upbringing of the Athenian military and political male élite, and so his conception of the appropriate doings that would flower into the appropriate virtues was appropriately conditioned by that goal. (He thought the idea that boys might learn to cook derisory.) I have argued that the sort of doing that schools prepare us for is, appropriately, servile. Moralised servility is still servility; and the attempt coercively to moralise servility will multiply cynicism and the motive to reject or revolt. This revolt, especially among the boys, is already an old rumble. Despite and in some ways because of the increasing confinements of their lives, young people have been for at least two generations liberal individualists by persuasion, as inured to their instructors' moralism as they are to their daily dose of Jesus, Abraham or Mohammed. While their friendships and animosities, their sharings and possessiveness, are as stable as ever, they conceive of freedom, individuality and community in terms largely antithetical to those articulated in the patri-matriarchal discourses of school, whose ties they cannot wait to rip off. Their playfulness, their imagination, their idealism, their creativity, their will to potency and recognition largely denied, their cognitive, contributive, aesthetic and sensory faculties largely stultified or denied expression, they engage in a kind of virtual and vicarious life of heroic excitement, power and passion, characterised by an almost ritualised mistrust of adults who, with no title to respect or devotion, seek to rule their lives. In a long life of learning, there will be a place for schools and classrooms, but until that place has been shifted, they will retain their disquieting and paralysing image in the minds of most who have passed through their doors.

I claimed a kind of innate complex of moral potential consequent on our common humanity. With that goes the idea that, while it can be atrophied or twisted, there is a capacity to see, respond to, and reflect on not Right and Wrong, as some spookily abstract rival commanders, but the rights and wrongs enmeshed in the situations we characteristically confront. This is not to deny the vicious and less lovely things that are part of our makeup; it is to deny the claim of the moralistic regimentalists that it is by *force-majeure* and preaching that morality gets introduced. No amount of guilt-tripping or shaming, congratulating or condemning, can substitute for an absence or shortfall of educative, ethically charged, experience in the densities, responsibilities, vulnerabilities and conflictual subtleties of everyday life. Ageist discourse has used the idea of helpless innocence in playing the protective governess over young people's lives, while turning the screw on the gates of their confinement. Appealing to a different focus-group, it has used the ideology of diminutive savagery to conceal the fostering by authoritarian constrictions of the very wild-child tendencies they then offer themselves to suppress. Being small, innately trustful and ineradicably vulnerable, children are open to all sorts of abuse, neglect and coercion. But these frailties are the other side of their systematically ignored potentialities. In an age where we do not need to protect western children from the drudgery of the loom or the factory or the chimney, we need to 'introduce' them with love and gentleness, into the give-and-take of an inter-generational human world. At the moment, our child-minders are thinking of ways of keeping them quiet in the waiting-room – the waiting-room to what?

Chapter 6

A Moral Fix

Carole Cox

The prevalent concern that teachers and schools address themselves to the moral education of the young has always been apparent but more recently this concern has become a desperate anxiety, fuelled by particular incidents, for example the Jamie Bulger case. All too often, this concern has been expressed in the unfortunately simplistic or crude terms – that, given the will, educators can prevent cruelty, violence, sadism, or any other nefarious practice or attitude towards others by the obvious means of 'teaching the difference between right and wrong'. There have been various species of 'outcry' in the tabloid press, and in the so-called 'quality' press, about the depths to which the young have sunk and how education, by which is meant compulsory schooling, is singularly ill-equipped to deal with the sophisticated temptations of life for the young person, both outside and inside school. There have been suggestions that lessons in morals might solve this problem. However, in our search for certainty and the comfort that it brings, which we particularly seek when we are afraid of the young and *for* the young, we can forget that easy answers, the 'quick fixes' of cliché, are no use. I want to offer a very long slow fix – to do with getting the young to engage with literature and with the ideas that it explores.

It is not new to suggest that literature can be a vehicle for moral education. Frequently politicians and public figures, including Prince Charles, allude to the significance of the 'canon', that is to the literary tradition which includes Chaucer, Shakespeare and Dickens, which will give children a sense of their heritage and help them to take a pride in that heritage. Although the canon is important and the sense of a tradition is significant in our understanding of literature and ourselves, it is vital that tradition is seen as changing and responsive to the new and innovative. Traditions should be living presences rather than a set of stultifying conventions if we are to be able to engage the young with conceptions of the moral. There can be room for Christopher Marlowe and Hanif Kureishi, Dickens and Meera Syal, Emily Bronte and Toni Morrison. All the aforementioned are part of traditions, plural, and re-make and re-model traditions also.

The concern for tradition centres upon a desire to provide a structure for the young to operate within and a heritage which they can inherit and can feel underpins their understanding of the world. This desire for a structure entails that when we express our concerns about the moral education of the young, we can find ourselves wanting children to know what the rules are and how to apply those rules. Unfortunately, there is no set of tablets of stone on which these rules are inscribed. Instead, moral situations are specific and particular, concrete and local. They require us to respond to these particulars, rather than to obey a rule or maxim. When a person, John, is lying in the gutter and another person, Sue, goes to his aid, enquires how he feels, it is rarely as a result of thinking 'I should be a good neighbour' but instead is a kind of instinct to do good – to be virtuous. For this reason, a good model of moral education is one which involves inculcating the virtues. For example, a young child, who has loving parents who attempt to be virtuous themselves, who attends a school where consideration and concern for others is part of the ethos, will have the disposition to be virtuous. She will want approval, loving affectionate regard for her actions.

Parents, therefore, reward kindness, compassion, consideration with approval, and by so doing instil a set of virtues – consideration, kindness and compassion – in children.

Furthermore, in such a moral education, parents wish their children to do what 'feels' right for them, to take account of what is good for the child as well as what is good behaviour on the part of the child. It is a strength of the education programmes aimed at preventing child abuse that children are encouraged to 'go with' their feelings of self-worth, that they are taught that, although they are children, if they do not feel safe or happy they are quite right to tell an adult to 'push off'. A more absolute sense of respect for one's elders, such as that often promoted by those who wish children to 'know the difference between right and wrong', would make this a very difficult position for a child to adopt. Such a view of moral education is one which makes it a grasping of rules similar to a learning of the Catechism, where the authority of the person inculcating the rules and the authoritative nature of the rules themselves take on considerable importance. A preferable vision is one of moral education as a nuanced understanding that much of moral response takes the form of 'it depends'. If a child always respects adults then she may find herself being made to do immoral things, sexual or otherwise. A more sensitive ethic involves considerations like the following: usually respect elders but in some circumstances follow your own instincts. Some people might want to argue that this moral position is far too vague. This latter idea, of taking particular circumstances into account, makes morality a much more risky business: one that adults might be able to cope with but hard for those who wish to teach their young – offspring or pupils – 'the difference between right and wrong'. The latter should be clear and simple: this seems to be what we want.

The emphasis though is on 'seems'. Children (and adults) may find rules comforting, in the sense that there are parameters set which make the world a place easier to understand. A relevant anecdote comes to mind here. Susan, a member of the Socialist Workers' Party, was concerned about a friend, Janet, who was beaten up by her husband. This friend received a lot of help and support from the Battered Wives Centre. The workers at the centre took the view that Janet was the victim of a patriarchical society: that is, men take out their frustrations on women. Susan, seeking a Marxist solution, was unhappy with this and so she phoned up the headquarters of the SWP to ask what her view of the feminism of the Battered Wives Centre should be. She was told that the rule is that class explains such behaviour. Working class men, rather than being oppressors themselves, are as oppressed as working class women, and she must persuade Janet of the truth of this. This true story illustrates the weakness of seeking rules when pondering how to live well. Metaphorically we are encouraging the young to phone up the Headquarters of ethics, to find out what the rules are and then apply them rather than to reflect upon the particulars of the case for themselves.

It is because moral life is much more likely to offer dilemmas than issues easily resolved by applications of rule that a better model of moral education is needed. This must emphasise the cultivation of the disposition to be virtuous. The central notion here is one of growth, development towards moral maturity, whereby one's inclination is to do right because it has become habitual. Habits, such as the habit to be concerned for others, become so thoroughly ingrained that there is no conscious effort to behave well. Such habits can be fostered in education. This is not to deny that there will be dilemmas and moral conflicts when simple good habits will not be sufficient. I will return to these occasions later in this chapter.

In seeking moral growth such as I depict, there is a central place for literature. By reading we understand much more fully what it is to lead good lives for ourselves and others. Even in the early stages of inculcating good habits in the young, stories and tales can benefit our teaching. For example, in discussing *Burglar Bill* with the very young we can draw attention to the way in which he changes his habits, turning from the life of crime to that of being a baker! *Charlie and the Chocolate Factory* contains ample evidence of the perils of indulging in greedier habits. Stories, poems, plays engage with what it is to lead a good life, the good for us and for others being inextricably linked. When one teaches literature, in talking about the words on the page, the characters in novels and plays, young people are being given the opportunity to consider what it is to lead a good life or a bad life.

Such considerations of good and bad lives are central to the discussion of a text such as *Edward II* by Christopher Marlowe. The young have to address a number of moral quandaries which go to the heart of their own preconceptions. The play tells the story of Edward's love for a man, Gaveston, a love which ultimately leads to the enmity of his wife and her collusion with Mortimer in rebellion. Both Gaveston and Edward are murdered, Edward in a particularly horrific manner. I taught this play to a group of boys and girls of varying cultural backgrounds which included three boys who were very ambivalent about homosexuality. Discussing the play enabled them to express that ambivalence and indeed overcome certain prejudices against those of a different sexuality. This was fostered by the very structure of the play in that Marlowe portrays Edward and his lover Gaveston so that we feel disapproval initially and then gradually Marlowe depicts their fall alongside the rise of their enemies. Issues which are taboo in a secular society, let alone for young Muslim people, regarding marital fidelity as well as homosexuality, have to be addressed when discussing Marlowe's play. This is because he shows how Edward taunts the Queen, his wife, Isabella, about his relationship with his 'minion' and yet makes the audience sympathise with the male lovers when they are destroyed by her. Two years of discussion of this play saw marked changes in attitude. At first Tim, Curtis and Mohammed expressed vehement dislike of studying such a text. At the end of the two years they expressed an equally strongly-felt understanding of the miseries of the major characters.

Edward II was written in the sixteenth century and is therefore long ago and far away enough, as well as vividly created enough, to allow students to face up to significant issues in a 'safe' way. Boys especially find it difficult to discuss moral issues because inevitably there is discussion of emotion and feeling which boys are socialised to eschew rather than admit to. Therefore, it is especially important that boys learn to 'use' literature or that literature can be 'used' with them to address the challenges and conflicts morality inevitably involves.

Such challenges and conflicts are endemic to the study of literature because life can be conceived of as a narrative: actions and circumstances bring consequences and possibilities in their wake. Books are narratives – often of moral quests and moral journeys. To share the narrative of the novel is to enrich our understanding of our own narrative quest. When young people think about their lives and about how to approach them, it is very helpful to compare their ideas to those of others. The central moral question is: what is it to lead a good life? In the narrative structure of the novel the consequences and dilemmas posed by this central question unfold in such a way as to illuminate young people's own shaping of their narrative, the structure of their own story. Philosophers from Aristotle to Alasdair MacIntyre have perceived the narrative as a rich way to explore ethics. In a novel like *David Copperfield* the hero's growth from childhood to maturity involves many moral dilemmas, uncertainties and conflicts, not least centring upon the fascinating and corrupt Steerforth and the friendship and love he offers the hero. In encountering these and discussing them with other young people and with the teacher, pupils are able to encounter parallels to their own conflicts. Friendships, especially with the unsuitable and delectable people who Mum and Dad disapprove of, are often the greatest cause of temptation, after all.

This very issue has arisen in discussions with young people, particularly young Muslims, where obedience to parental authority is very firmly ingrained and where the friendships offered by school or college can be exciting and forbidden. Other students may drink alcohol and smoke, both forbidden in Islam; other students may be of a different religion and therefore not considered suitable partners for a Muslim boy or girl. The conflicts David Copperfield experiences between his good angel, Agnes, and his bad one, Steerforth, enable young people to explore their own anxieties here despite the differences culturally.

This is because we can 'read' our lives better if we can read books: if one can really *read*. One becomes eager to be enriched, one can pick up clues, perceive the connections, by reading. One starts to see how this reading of one novel can be deepened by reading of another. After all, part of the pleasure of Salinger's *The Catcher in the Rye* is its stated difference from *David Copperfield*. These books about young people growing up and having to make hard ethical decisions are invaluable. They offer us a richer sense of what it is to be a person in a baffling world, faced with decisions of difficult kinds.

What is most fundamental of all, however, to any reading of literature and of life is that sense of imaginative sympathy which is vital to morality. If I cannot imagine how it might feel to be in great pain, grief, sorrow, then I am unable to help another in pain, and more importantly I may feel able to hurt or damage another. If I can think and understand the force of 'Supposing I was burned, kicked, shouted at. How would you feel?', then I am less likely to inflict harm on another. We need to develop the imagination in order to think like this and this is precisely what reading books can do.

In developing imagination as readers we develop a vocabulary of moral distinctions and discrimination. We need to have particular words and expressions at our disposal if we are going to be able to make finer moral discriminations. If I have no concept of temptation, I will not understand what it is to do what I know is wrong and violates my principles. If I simply know what the word means because I looked it up in the dictionary, I am less likely to apply that understanding than if I have read *David Copperfield* and have engaged with Steerforth's own agonisings regarding Emily as well as David's torments regarding his friend's conduct and David's love for him.

The fact that resonant language and imagery, and concretely realised context, enables us to make more discriminating moral distinctions, is no more evident than in the conflicts which make up the moral world that is *Edward II*. It is the conflict between Edward's desire to be a good king and his love for the politically unsuitable Gaveston that shapes the vital moral issues which resonate throughout the play: the realm of public obligation versus the desire for private happiness. Young people are brought to consider these issues and to engage with moral dilemmas – vital to any moral education and understanding.

The much more sophisticated business of engaging with moral dilemma and conflict is enormously enriched by involvement with literature. There are particularly pressing problems for the educator when considering such conflicts within a multiracial society, as I have indicated already.

These conflicts have led to suggestions that teachers *cannot* educate the young morally. Because young persons come from different cultures and traditions, it has been mooted that distinctions and differentiations between moral stances cannot be made without prejudice. This view recognises that moral judgements are shaped and operate within areas which involve conflicts of a religious and cultural nature. It is not sufficient to argue as a result of this recognition that moral education should only be addressed at home, in the church, in the mosque or temple. Indeed, that there are conflicts makes it even more imperative that moral education takes place in schools as well as within the wider community. It is wrong-headed to argue that Sharon cannot criticise the actions of Avnee because she comes from a different tradition. Teachers may hesitate to condemn the *fatwah* regarding Salman Rushdie when half of their students come from a Muslim background but they should not 'duck' the issue.

However, it is surely vital that the young address these conflicts in as detached and engaged a way as possible. As I suggested earlier, literature enables the young to involve themselves with real issues and real moral conflicts in a 'safe' way because the convention of fiction gives a distance and life-like depiction offers sensitive analogies to our own uncertainties and moral concerns. The likelihood of offending others is also diminished by this distance, as we can fall back on 'it is a book that we are discussing'.

An excellent example of a discussion centred upon moral conflict is a fascinating debate between two pupils which focused upon Heathcliff's behaviour in *Wuthering Heights*. Heathcliff behaves with considerable cruelty towards a number of characters in the novel. One view is that this is understandable given his own ill-treatment as a child. One could say that Heathcliff behaves as he does because he is a victim of abuse. This view was put by one person, Caryl, with considerable passion and with consideration of the kinds of arguments that we might deploy when considering the moral case of the person who has only received unkindness and therefore knows no better. The moral case might be 'to know all is to forgive all'. The other pupil, Julia, put as compelling a moral case that Heathcliff's awareness of the cruelty that can be visited upon the young and vulnerable made it even more incumbent upon him to behave decently. Concomitant with this was Julia's view that it was morally reprehensible to excuse violence by reference to one's upbringing. I am not claiming that these issues were resolved. They were aired and discussed at considerable length and with great passion by students of various abilities and from a range of backgrounds – African-Caribbean, Asian and white. The novel provided the distance and the engagement to make this possible.

I suspect that many concerned with discipline, order and punishment – the traditional answers to the question of how we teach the recalcitrant young – will find my suggestions that literature is invaluable in a moral education 'woolly and wet'. However, I have found, working with inner-city young people of all abilities and mostly from poor backgrounds, that the young are good and that they often humble those who wish to guide them!

As I argued earlier, books provide the 'slow fix' over the years, in that they open vistas for the young and the young have a keen sense of the ways in which literature offers different versions and different visions of how to live. The conflicts and risks of what it is to live well or live badly are made present to the young in literature. Young people's responses to these con- flicts and risks are grounds for hope and not for despair about the moral lives of the young and the world which they will be shaping in the future.

Chapter 7

Innate Morality:
A Psychoanalytic Approach
to Moral Education

Michael Rustin

Contemporary debate about the crisis of morality seems readily to assume that moral dispositions are fragile and unreliable aspects of human nature. They are said to be in grave danger of being undermined and stripped away by the siren voices of individualism, hedonism, and greed. 'Morality' is implicitly seen as a superficial veneer of habits and principles, which needs to be continually reinforced by the forces of civilisation lest they be swept away by raging antisocial desires and passions.

In this situation, two responses to the moral crisis are commonly offered. One is intensified coercion. The other, the occasion for this book, is a demand for moral education. Resocialisation is to be achieved by a combination of the threat and application of force, and by pedagogy.

Thus, in the domain of coercion, there are calls for stiffer sentences, more imprisonment, 'zero-tolerance' policing, curfews for the young, and sweeping the homeless off the streets. (The signs are, however, that New Labour in office may be less punitive than its attitudes in opposition.) There are loud statements of outrage at individual acts which seem to threaten the moral order, especially when children are affected as victims or perpetrators. The significance of children in all this is that they seem to indicate that new boundaries of depravity have been crossed. There has also been the preoccupation with 'sleaze', and the pursuit and public shaming of delinquency, whether financial or sexual, by figures in public life. The climax of this demand to clean up public life came with the successful challenge to Neil Hamilton in the Tatton constituency by Martin Bell, most recently distinguished for his insistence on the moral obligations of journalists in the reporting of civil wars like those of the former Yugoslavia.

In the sphere of education, there is the demand that moral standards should be taught in schools, even as part of the formal curriculum. The self-same teachers, whose general inadequacies and lack of competence have been the theme of so many years of political denunciation, are now called into action as teachers of moral enlightenment to the children. The implicit idea seems to be that morality consists of a self-evident set of rules and precepts. It is because these have been lost sight of, or taken for granted within an educational system misled by the permissive assumptions of the 1960s, that pupils have failed to learn morality. The model of didactic learning invoked here is related to the ideas of whole-class pedagogy which are also being insisted on in the more instrumental areas of the curriculum. Learning, on these assumptions, is not a process of discovery, pushed forward by curiosity, puzzlement, or the enjoyment of a shared task, but the imparting of a corpus of facts, procedures, and rules to the hitherto empty minds of the children. Moral dispositions, it seems to be believed, can and should be transmitted in this way.

'In this life, we want nothing but Facts, Sir; nothing but Facts!'

The speaker, and the schoolmaster, and the third grown-up person present, all backed a little, and swept with their eyes the inclined plane of little vessels then and there arranged in order, ready to have imperial gallons of facts poured into them until they were full to the brim.
(Charles Dickens, *Hard Times*, 1854)

Underlying these coercive and didactic responses to the problems of morality is an implicit view of human nature as innately selfish, except where social and moral restraints are laid upon it. The 'selfishness' and 'greed' which are defined as a major social problem, 'out there' in society, seem thus to have crept 'inside' as part of the frame of definitions through which this problem has been diagnosed. Certain ways of treating the problem then seem to follow from the diagnosis.

The development of this state of affairs has in truth been a complex social process. An ideology which asserted the productive benefits of 'enterprise' and self-interest, against the 'dependency culture' of the welfare state, was the moving force behind the major institutional changes of 'Thatcherism', and some associated change in English culture. Some sections of society became less protected against the incidence of insecurity and poverty than they had formerly been. It has been demonstrated that rates of crime, delinquency and family breakdown are related to levels of unemployment, despite the late government's great antipathy to this idea. And at the other end of the income spectrum, there has been a greater tolerance of huge disparities of wealth, even when it is clear that large gains made by some are clearly the consequence (for example, through downsizing and redundancy, or through the under-pricing of privatised public assets) of large losses to others. The 'moral disorders' of crime at both ends of the economic spectrum (uncontrollable children in sink schools, delinquent traders in the financial system, or MPs who were bribed to ask Parliamentary questions) are consequences of an ideology which devalued social obligations and responsibilities.

Within the framework of this ideology, which retained a dominant position in the national life until the recent election, there was no admissible solution to the problems it gave rise to but sanctions, and the fear of them which moral education was probably mainly intended to instil. It was the idea that people might basically be constructed in different, more sociable, more co-operative ways, which had been cast out by the assumptions behind an authoritarian market society.

It is this situation which has made the responses to signs of breakdown of moral order so contradictory and irrational. The abridgement of childhood dependency involved in bringing down the age of criminal responsibility, or in increasing the sentences of the boys who killed James Bulger (treating them to all intents and purposes as if they were already adults) is one example. The contradictory role of the press is another, since it has simultaneously incited sexual transgression (by its titillating displays and reporting of sexual adventures, for example those of David Mellor or members of the Royal Family), yet also delighted in exposing and denouncing these. The figure of Max Clifford, who has created a lucrative niche for himself as a conduit for such stories, yet justifies himself as a moralist and supporter of New Labour, is emblematic.

If those concerned with moral education do not wish to become just another symptom of the problem, they need to take a more fundamental view of it. At the root is the question of human nature, and our beliefs about it. There are more and less pessimistic views of this within our philosophical tradition. Current political thinking represents the (unacknowledged) ascendancy of a particularly pessimistic and conservative version of this, closest to Thomas Hobbes though without his illusion-less realism. Different traditions – from Aristotle, Rousseau, Hegel, and Wittgenstein, for example – support a view of humankind as more innately social, as constituted not merely by base passions kept in order only by external sanctions, but by innate identifications as members of social groups larger than the individual. There is no space to go into these different traditions here, but it is important to point out that debates about morality take for granted fundamental presuppositions of this kind, whether they are acknowledged or not.

I shall argue that morality is innate in human nature, not an external superimposition of norms and standards upon it. One does not need to go further than our ordinary language for evidence that this is the case. Common language is saturated with moral descriptions, concerning the qualities of persons, and their motivations and actions. We describe individuals as, for example, sincere or hypocritical, kind or indifferent, sensitive or thick-skinned, fair-minded or self-interested, selfish or generous, and in doing so we continually make judgements about their consideration of others. It is regard for the reasonable claims of other persons, or the lack of it, which marks the 'moral' dimension in such descriptions. Hardly a conversation about persons is imaginable that does not involve the scrutiny and assessment of their 'moral' qualities.

These are not the only qualities which interest us in other persons – their beauty, intelligence, humour, malice, or general likeability also figure in our interest or otherwise in them. Our language allows us to frame such descriptions as objective ones, allowing us to distinguish statements about the real attributes of someone from a mere expression of our own personal feelings about them. The point of describing someone as having certain qualities (being humorous, generous, etc.) is that such descriptions are recognisable to anyone, not merely to oneself. For someone to be a kind person is more than for them to be kind to me, although we may well present such a fact as evidence for this larger characterisation. To ascribe moral qualities ('kind' is in fact one such, on any broad view of the ethical), is essentially to offer a description which is presented as valid from more than one person's view of view.

Our discourse about persons is, in other words, inherently normative. Moral assessments and evaluations seem to be built into its very structure, from the beginnings of children's use of language.

The Contribution of Psychoanalysis

Our ordinary language and its use in everyday life provide grounds for believing that moral dispositions, in ourselves and others, are our normal expectation of persons. It is indeed difficult to imagine social relations being conducted without them. But in this chapter I develop a more specific argument, about the contribution which psychoanalytic thinking can bring to our understanding of these questions.[1] Psychoanalytic investigations of human nature have been among the most profound which have been undertaken in this century. One particular contribution which psychoanalysis has made has been to reintegrate into human understanding domains of emotion, and in particular unconscious states of mind, which had become difficult to think about within the dominant scientific and rationalist paradigms. Psychoanalysis sought to find a secular language to describe and account for fundamental states of feeling which had until the end of the nineteenth century belonged mainly to the language and practice of religion. Psychoanalysis sought to provide a developmental account of the origins of love and hate, and of the nature of the moral dispositions and disorders which had always been central to both ethical and religious thought – states of mind such as envy, destructiveness, narcissism, and so on. Melanie Klein entitled two of her books *Envy and Gratitude,* and *Love, Hate and Reparation.*

I shall argue that the later development of the psychoanalytic tradition provides a useful theoretical container for the idea that human beings are innately social, that is to say are dependent on and preoccupied with the well-being of others from their earliest months of life. By 'later development' I refer to the theory of 'object relations', developed by Klein, Winnicott, Fairbairn and others, which built on the discoveries of Freud but modified them in significant ways (Greenberg and Mitchell, 1983). This theory rehabilitates an idea of innate relatedness which was displaced from the centre of understanding by both a dominant model of behaviour based on individual self-interest, and by the separation of reason and emotion within the emerging human sciences, whose effect was the marginalisation of affective life. The dominant human sciences of psychology, economics and political science based themselves on a model of rational individual self-interest, and attempted to construct a model of stable social order on that foundation. Moral philosophy in Britain, under the competing sway of Kant and utilitarianism, largely accepted these assumptions, though with a minority of dissenting voices which has become more numerous in later years (Foot, 1978; MacIntyre, 1981; Williams, 1985; Lovibond, 1983). The argument being developed here is a form of 'naturalistic ethics', based on a psychoanalytic view of human nature. More affect-rich, holistic reflections on human nature were more easily pursued in the humanities, for example in the study of literature, than in fields dominated by scientific approaches.

However, the later development of psychoanalysis in Britain is of moral interest not only for these broad foundational reasons. An additional contribution of psychoanalytic thinking is that it enables us to differentiate two radically different states of moral feeling, both within individuals as they develop from infancy, and in their social forms. The model of moral development set out by Melanie Klein and her successors is based on a contrast between what she called the 'paranoid-schizoid' position, in which others are perceived essentially as objects of fear and hostility, and the 'depressive position', in which love for and dependence on others is acknowledged. 'Depressive anxiety' is evoked by concern about the well-being of the other, whereas 'persecutory anxiety' is focused on perceived threats to the well-being of the self (Klein, 1986).

This model is a powerful one, which orders and explains complex configurations of moral feeling, both within individuals and in societies, as we shall see. First, however, it is necessary to say something more about the evolution of moral understanding within the psychoanalytic tradition.

Psychoanalysis and the Moral Sense: a Brief History

From its beginnings, psychoanalysis was preoccupied with the origins and nature of morality. Freud understood that moral dispositions became internalised very early in childhood development, in his view through the experience of the Oedipal situation and the necessity for the child to renounce its omnipotent claims on its parent of opposite gender. The strength of Freud's view was its recognition of the repressed, and thus irrational, element in moral prohibition. The civilised morality imposed at the behest of this internalised superego was a very mixed blessing, so far as Freud was concerned, maintaining 'social order' only at a high price in instinctual denial and non-recognition. He favoured a less repressive approach to child-rearing, and to sexuality more generally, holding that with greater recognition of unconscious desires and needs, a more reality-based accommodation to the needs of the self and others could be achieved. 'Morality' could not be taken at its own self-proclaimed value once its roots in repression and denial were understood. Freud's contribution to thinking about morality was thus mainly negative and deconstructive (as Nietzsche's was), though it was nevertheless essential in calling into question the repressive moral precepts of the prevailing conservative social order.

But its limitation lies in Freud's unduly egoistic model of the desiring self. Desire for objects, and identification with them, rather than concern for their well-being, are still the central building blocks of Freud's developmental theory. Freud took on the scientistic aspirations of his contemporaries which were later rejected or qualified by his successors. In a parallel way, his assumptions about motivation took on some of the individualist assumptions of contemporary liberal ways of thinking.[2] These were also questioned and modified by later analysts formed by more familial, feminised and organic conceptions of human nature.

Freud had been concerned to expose the irrational, repressive quality of much moral thinking, whose origin lay in fear of the father at the Oedipal stage. Freud's aim was to lessen the severity of such repression, and to make possible a fuller acknowledgement of and understanding of the range of human desires. Klein's view of the moral sense was more positive, in that she saw at least one aspect of it – the 'depressive aspect' – as founded not on fear of retribution but on concern for the loved object, and on anxiety about the damage which the self might inflict upon it.

According to Klein, the origins of moral feeling lay prior to awareness of the oedipal situation, in the earliest relationship of the infant to its mother or mother-figure. Klein views the infant as subject to overwhelming desires for and demands upon its primary object. Contentiously, Klein ascribed to the infant a rather complex 'internal world' in which parental figures are perceived in intensely passionate terms, feelings of love and hate alternating rapidly in response in part to the frustration and satisfaction experienced by the infant. One crucial aspect of the 'parenting' of infants, according to this theory, is to take in and modulate these intense feelings, thus enabling the infant gradually to learn to distinguish reality from its own feelings about it, and to develop a mind in which thought can take place. Where parents are unable, for whatever reason, to provide a sufficient level of emotional responsiveness, there is risk that serious developmental arrest or disorder in the infant may take place.

The 'paranoid-schizoid position' in Klein's model of development is a structure in which fear and aggression are felt to be unbearable to the self, and are projected outwards, initially on to the primary caregivers who are the main objects of infantile desire, love and anger. Klein's idea is that the infant is then persecuted, in fantasy, by all this negative emotion. Because the sources of the infant's pains and frustrations are at some moments hated, they are imagined to be full of hate for the infant. Although the theoretical apparatus being deployed here, of internal worlds, fantasy, projections etc., may seem highly conjectural, the essential mental process is surely familiar. Hostility directed towards others leads to our imagining them to be full of hatred for ourselves, whether we have evidence for this or not.[3] This is the essence of the 'paranoid-schizoid position', which is both a developmental phase and a pattern of feeling which remains latent throughout life. In this state of mind good and bad become constructed as the divided aspects of the primary object to which the self is attached. In the formation of the primitive superego, this splitting is also directed inwards, and the self is constituted as having good and bad parts. Where hatred predominates in a personality, not others but also the self will be conceived in negative terms. There is no basis, either inside or outside, for the development of relations of love or trust, or such basis as there is is liable to be constantly overwhelmed by negative feeling.

Klein thought that these early and cruel psychic patterns gave rise to an equally harsh moral structure, a retributive morality in which hate and destructiveness are fantasised as always liable to be repaid in kind. Where this morality becomes rationalised as a set of beliefs, it corresponds to the law of the talion, violence justly met with violence. Klein's primary discovery here was of an innate propensity to persecution and guilt. She found that moral life originates in a very early and harsh superego which functions initially through the radical splitting of good and bad aspects of the self and others. In this 'paranoid-schizoid' state of mind, the self is idealised, the other seen as threatening. A vicious spiral of internal and external persecution can be set up, if the personality fails to develop beyond this paranoid-schizoid stage.

In benign, normal forms of childhood development, destructive feelings are contained by more loving states of mind, though they are never entirely absent. But excessive frustration, or outright cruelty, or sometimes constitutional factors, can lead to a predominance of the negative, and to the formation of personalities beset by persecution and hatred.

However, Klein argued, personalities normally *do* develop beyond the paranoid-schizoid stage. In normal development the parent's or primary care-giver's capacity to tolerate the infant's demands, and to hold at a tolerable level its frustration and anxiety, allow the integration of different feelings within the personality. The infant comes to recognise that the 'object' (attributes of a person) which it sometimes hates is the same as the one it also loves. This greater psychic integration leads to recognition that the primary object is itself susceptible to pain and harm. Love for the object contributes to its being valued, and to becoming an object of concern in its own right. A different quality of moral feeling arises from this capacity to acknowledge and value the other in herself. This is what is meant by the 'depressive position', and this is the emotional context in which the capacity for remorse, grief, and reparation develop. Psychic 'splitting' is lessened, since there is a capacity to tolerate the imperfect both in others and the self. In other words, Klein allows back in the recognition of the other as foundational to morality.

The moral sensibility which arises from this more integrated personality formation is more tolerant, more devoted to the protection of objects, and more able to bear pain, loss and change, than the morality of the paranoid-schizoid position. The Kleinians sought through psychotherapeutic practice to understand how paranoid-schizoid anxieties could be recognised and reduced, and patients helped to move towards more psychically integrated and 'depressive' (and thus morally responsible) ways of functioning.

The concepts of 'paranoid-schizoid' and 'depressive' types of moral thinking are powerful ones, and I shall later show that they can have valuable applications to contemporary moral debate. But before elaborating these, it will be useful briefly to describe a third stage in the development of moral thinking within the British psychoanalytic tradition. The value of this contribution is in the attention it gives to the intractability of some destructive and negative states of mind (what in another vocabulary might be termed 'evil'). Where such unwelcome realities are not faced and understood, default to cruel and persecutory modes of dealing with what is held to lie outside the realm of understanding is all too likely. John Major's adjuration, in the context of the Bulger case, to 'condemn a little more and understand a little less', did not suggest that he believed that any useful understanding was possible.

This next stage in analytic thinking about moral states came about when certain Kleinian analysts encountered in their clinical practice intractable obstacles in some analysands to movement from paranoid-schizoid to depressive states of mind, the precondition of improved psychic health. A model of 'borderline states' (borderline, that is, between paranoid-schizoid and depressive positions), which was also termed 'narcissistic personality disorders', was evolved to explain these resistances to change (Steiner, 1993).

The most severe form of these disorders is what Rosenfeld (1987) called destructive narcissistic organisation (distinguishing this from the less damaging form of libidinal narcissism). In this structure, the personality is dominated by negative and hateful feelings directed against both its objects and against good parts of the self. Rosenfeld developed the vivid concept of an internal psychic organisation which functions in the manner of 'a powerful gang dominated by a leader, who controls all the members of the gang to see that they support one another in making the criminally destructive work all the more effective and powerful.'

Donald Meltzer (1973) had earlier developed a similar idea, in his paper 'Terror, Persecution and Dread'. Meltzer's argument takes as given that the personality in infancy is constituted in part by its internalised identifications with fantasied parental figures, which persist as unconscious templates of the personality. In extreme paranoid-schizoid states, dominated by destructive projections, the personality may imagine itself as having caused grave damage to its objects. The worst imaginable damage is the destruction of new babies that the parents may produce, which may be wished dead both as potential rivals, and as symbols, in this hate-filled state of mind, of the parents' envied creativity. Thus, the 'terror' of the paper's title refers to the terror of the 'dead babies' destroyed in fantasy by the self. It is this state of terror from which the omnipotent gang-like mental formation protects the personality, in Meltzer's view. This state of mind, which of course is primarily observed by these analysts in the clinical setting of the transference, protects the self from recognition of objects who have been, or would be, destroyed by hate, and who would also exact retribution for the hatred directed towards them, if they were allowed psychically to exist.

The psychic metaphor of the gang in Rosenfeld's and Meltzer's work is a resonant one. It serves both to explain mental formations by reference to what we already know or imagine of real gangs and it also informs in psychic terms our understanding of such gangs and their fascination for us.

These ideas enable us to explain some of the more intractable features of delinquent and criminal behaviour. They enable us to understand how an apparent commitment or addiction to evil can arise, as a defence against projected persecutory states of mind unmitigated by love or trust. These ideas also explain why change in these personalities is so exceptionally difficult to achieve, since its beginnings expose the personality to recognition of the psychically intolerable damage it has already done, and the danger, in fantasy, to which this damage exposes it.

Although the psychoanalytically-informed are sometimes thought to be rather 'soft' towards criminality, it should be clear that these approaches take very seriously the destructive elements of human nature, and the difficulties in bringing about change once personalities come to be unconsciously dominated by hatred.

What this psychoanalytic account does presuppose, however, is that the personality is essentially structured, through infancy and later developmental experiences, by its internal relation to others. These relations will be based on some mixture of love and hate. More 'depressive' states of mind bring a capacity to identify with and feel concern for the well-being of significant others. In persecutory states of mind, only the interests of the self count, and others are viewed primarily as objects of hate and fear.

Every person of course experiences both of these states of mind, in oscillation, but in different balances with one another.

These personality structures are defined, in late Kleinian thinking, not only by the predominance of love and hate within them but also by their relationship to reality and understanding itself. A major contribution of Wilfred Bion to this tradition was his development of Melanie Klein's idea of a primary 'epistemophilic instinct' into an understanding of the psychic preconditions of a propensity to tolerate and seek knowledge of reality.[4] Some early psychic integration is necessary to sustain the development of a mind (childhood autism and psychosis are thus possible outcomes of extreme environmental deficit). But, once formed, the mind can be diverted to the service of destructiveness, in the phenomena of envy and lies, for example.

Moral Environments

What follows from this psychoanalytic account of the origin and function of moral dispositions and sentiments, from the point of view of moral well-being, and more specifically of moral education? Two implications will be suggested. The first of these is more general, and concerns the conditions in which moral development and learning can take place. The second develops the distinction between 'paranoid-schizoid' and 'depressive' moralities, and suggests ways in which this can inform contemporary moral debate.

The key psychoanalytic idea is that the origins of the moral capacity are located in the context of primary relationships, from infancy onwards. The guiding assumption is that where appropriate qualities of care are provided (care which responds to emotional as well as physical needs), the great majority of individuals will develop normal capacities for love and moral concern, admixed with more destructive impulses but usually in containable ways. Whilst rivalry, for example with siblings in the family, and with their symbolic equivalents in play-group, classroom, or friends, is a normal state of mind, parental and quasi-parental commitment to each child, and fairness towards them, normally mitigates its severity, and enables sharing and reciprocity to develop through identification (Rustin, M. E. and M. J., 1985). The primary source of moral dispositions and capability lies in the provision of a 'good enough environment'.

What a 'good enough environment' means is one in which anxiety and its attendant destructive feelings are kept within tolerable bounds, and the loving and truth-seeking propensities of the self are given sufficient nourishment to support development. In these circumstances, psychic integration can take place, the uncertainties and challenges of reality can be faced and responsibility be taken for the consequences of actions and desires for other persons.

This is what is intended by the assertion in the title of this paper that morality is 'innate'. (Current work in neuroscience (Damasio, 1994) is indicating that there is an organic basis for emotional and moral capacities, though there is no space to elaborate this here.)

Moral qualities are thus nurtured largely by experience, and also, through identification, by example. The family is the most important setting for such experience, but the other major contexts of life – school, workplace, the larger community – are also formative. Indeed, these to some degree provide the preconditions for the benign functioning of families, since in external conditions of acute deprivation, insecurity or terror it is unlikely that families will be able to maintain internally benign conditions for emotional and moral development. Good later experiences in non-family settings can, however, to some degree compensate for insufficiencies in earlier family settings. What is crucial for moral development is the affective environment – the quality of relationships which are available to individuals.

Reflection and the elaboration of thought about moral questions – for example, the nature and extent of obligations, the appropriate sanctioning of deviancy, the formation of ideals and goals for the self – will be normal activities in good environments. The essence of moral learning is not intellectual subscription to abstract precepts, but a process of learning-within-a-situation, from experience and example, in which the implications and effects of feelings or actions can be reflected on with others. For example, moral issues attached to sexuality may be explored around experiences of pleasure, pain, and possible loss, and who suffers these.

Thus, moral dispositions are likely to be the outcome, more than the cause, of social relationships. It is the quality of these which we must attend to if we are concerned about moral breakdown.

Paranoid-Schizoid States of Mind

Where moral development fails, paranoid-schizoid states of mind, in both individuals and society, are likely to be the outcome. These states of mind are constituted not by the absence of moral feeling, but by its organisation in predominantly cruel and punitive ways. Where hatred and destructiveness are too potent to be contained or reflected on, they are projected outwards, into imagined or real enemies, and into categories of individuals who are chosen to bear psychic attributes and conditions which the rest of society cannot tolerate. Such projections, even though they are charged with unconscious anxieties, also have real effects and consequences. Those subject to stigma or hatred are likely to be influenced in material and psychic ways by these attributions.[5]

A 'zero degree' of moral feeling is a rare state of affairs according to the psychoanalytic theory set out here. Mostly, what appears to be moral blankness is better understood as a state of extreme defendedness, the projection into others of all awareness of pain or damage. The sufferings of victims enable the perpetrator to avoid suffering. This may be a reason for the element of repetition compulsion involved in certain kinds of atrocity. Donald Winnicott, in his essay 'Psychoanalysis and the Sense of Guilt' (1965), suggests that those who commit crimes often do so in order to be punished. Minor kinds of delinquent act are committed 'in an unconscious attempt to make sense of guilt feeling'. In more severe cases, it is the sense of guilt itself which is repressed, and the criminal is engaged in a 'desperate attempt to feel guilty' (which is usually unsuccessful, Winnicott added).

If families, schools, workplaces, neighbourhoods, even the larger political society, are the incubators of moral capacities, then moral capacities will fail when such institutions fail. The psychoanalytic model being used here formulates this process as one of 'containment'. Unless the anxieties incurred by the normal stresses of life are appropriately 'contained' within relationships and institutions which respect the value of individuals, they will generate destructive forms of psychic defence.

It is possible to see therefore how a more insecure and severely competitive social order will generate paranoid-schizoid forms of psychic organisation. Acute anxiety must be managed somehow, and violent forms of splitting in which negative feelings can be projected into some enemy or other, in reality or fantasy, are an effective defensive system. It is obvious that xenophobic hatred is directly related in its intensity to the degree of insecurity and anxiety suffered by a population, as we can see in the correlation between unemployment levels and the rise of racism in contemporary Europe. Civil conflicts, such as in Northern Ireland or the former Yugoslavia, are even more extreme examples, in which violence and terror become a self-perpetuating cycle. Physical boundaries between antagonistic groups, such as national frontiers, usually have a containing effect on such states of conflict, since at least the negative feelings are then pushed safely outside the community.

Truth is an early casualty of such paranoid-schizoid states of mind, public communication becoming instrumentalised as a weapon of interest, or even as a vehicle for the transmission of hatred. The widespread feeling in Britain that the political process had become a debased form of communication, in which truth-seeking was habitually subordinated to partisan advantage, was an interesting reflection of public attitudes to the social climate.

We can thus see that demands to 'remoralise' society, whether by the instruction or punishment of deviants, are liable to be themselves reflections of a paranoid-schizoid defensive system. As the sources of moral capability (what Durkheim called 'social solidarity') have been undermined by greater insecurity and more widespread anxiety, so the same political leadership which was responsible for this undermining responded in stridently prescriptive terms to the crisis its own changes had helped to bring about. This seemed to be more a symptom of than a solution to the problems.

Notably, however, the electorate voted largely against this offer of more of the same. Instead, it responded to evocations of a society in which there would be greater 'trust'. This has provided an opportunity to think about these issues of containment and solidarity in a more positive way.

If one wants a more 'ethical' society – that is, one in which people identify and empathise with others, and take responsibility for the consequences of their own actions – then one has to support the institutional preconditions for it. Families whose members are able to support the responsibilities of parenting, schools which are able to give their pupils the individual recognition that comes from individual attention, and work-places that create relations of trust with their employees, are such preconditions. Moral dispositions – norms of reciprocity – are unlikely to emerge when individuals do not feel recognised or supported by their social environment.[6]

It is much easier to facilitate moral development than to repair damage to personalities or communities once this has taken place. The reasons for this lie partly in the intractability of pathological defences once these have been adopted. Persecutory and persecuting structures do offer substantial defences against psychic pain, even though at others' cost. But an additional difficulty in achieving remedial change is the envy and jealousy felt by members of many communities at the idea that compensatory attention and care need to be given to the morally and emotionally damaged, if they are to have hope of recovery. In conditions of deprivation, it seems a poor reward, to those who have conformed to social norms, to see those who have not conformed being given any special consideration. Remedial institutions of any quality are subjected to intense projections of hatred towards those they are responsible for, and of resentment of any good that they manage to do them. Offenders must at all costs be punished, and any apparent 'softness' towards them ('holidays at the public expense', etc.) is vilified. Those charged with managing these public sentiments towards the deviant (social workers, teachers, even prison governors and judges) are liable to be attacked whatever they do.

Conclusion

The demand for prescriptive teaching of moral principles has recently functioned mainly as a mechanism of denial of the damage that is being done to moral capabilities and dispositions by the weakening of many social institutions, including the family (Hutton, 1997). Whilst there have been many demands that more attention be given to moral issues, this prescriptive climate has been largely inimical to rather than supportive of moral thinking.

There seems, however, in the new political climate to be an opportunity to think about these questions afresh, and to address the conditions which must be met if society and its members are to become more responsive to the needs of others, and to larger purposes than material self-interest. The psychoanalytic approach set out here provides one resource for rethinking the foundations of social life, and the sources of the moral dispositions on which it is based.

Notes

1.   Richard Wollheim's (1993) argument that Freud did not depart from but 'deepened, elaborated and contextualised' the theory of the mind embedded in ordinary language can be applied also to the psychoanalytic theory of morality.

2.   Standard accounts of Freud's ideas about morality are given by Rieff (1959) and Wollheim (1971).

3.   Thomas Hobbes understood that the self can feel as threatened by the harm it has inflicted, as by the harm it has suffered: 'To have done more hurt to a man than he can, or is willing to expiate, inclineth the doer to hate the sufferer. For he must expect revenge or forgiveness, both of which are hateful.' (Thomas Hobbes, Leviathan, 1651)

4.   By 'epistemophilic instinct', Klein meant the innate desire for knowledge, in the first instance sexual knowledge. Klein's work extended Freud's description of infantile sexual curiosity in his case histories (1909) in the direction of a broader theory of the origins of mind, which was then further developed by Bion. These ideas are referenced in Hinshelwood (1989).

5.   Richard Wilkinson's Unhealthy Societies (1996) provides evidence of the damage, reflected in the incidence of ill-health, of members of society subject to relative stigma and dis-esteem.

6.   This case is developed from an attachment theory perspective in S. Kraemer's and J. Roberts' The Politics of Attachment (1996).

Chapter 8

Moral Learning: a lifelong task

Bill Williamson

The argument developed in this chapter is this: morality is learned and moral learning is continuous throughout life. The elements of an individual's moral outlook may be inculcated in childhood, but these could never be sufficient to enable adults to understand the moral choices they continue to make throughout their adult lives. What people learn reflects the circumstances of their lives and the resources of moral understanding available to them. Given the truth of these propositions, the moral education of the young has to be based on a sound understanding of the moral dilemmas of adulthood and of the ways in which these change through time.

From this perspective, morality cannot fruitfully be viewed as an agreed code of values to which people more or less conform. Nor can it be seen as a divinely given framework of universally valid rules. It has to be seen instead as a socially constructed set of rules, values and sentiments which reflect the attempts of different groups of human beings in different cultures to do what they believe is 'good' or 'right'. One writer has suggested that the obligatory nature of a moral action derives from the prevailing sense of its 'rightness' (Collier, 1997). The rightness of an action, however, is not given: it is discovered within the frameworks of a culture which confer meaning and legitimacy on the different ways in which people resolve the dilemmas of living their lives in relationships with others. To seek to teach morality, either to children or adults, on the assumption that there are moral absolutes to be learned or that there is an agreed set of core moral values, is to prevent a full understanding of the nature of moral obligation and of the social arrangements within which it must be sustained.

The line of argument developed here is meant to challenge two conventional current views of morality and of moral education. One of these, reflected in the School Curriculum and Assessment Authority's (SCAA) report, *Spiritual and Moral Development* (1995), is the belief that there are moral absolutes. 'Schools', the report says, 'should be expected to uphold those values which contain moral absolutes' (p. 5). These include truthfulness, fidelity, respect for others, caring for others and individual responsibility. The case developed here is that while such values are important, they are not, however, in any reasonable sense of the word, absolute. It does not follow from this that all values are therefore relative.

In the report *Education for Adult Life* (1996) SCAA's Chief Executive, Dr. Nick Tate, described relativism as a dragon in need of slaying. The dragon of relativism is, however, no real threat. Indeed, it is far more serious to believe, as many delegates to SCAA's conference seemed to do, that the fundamental idea of 'objective moral truth' needs to be recovered as a defence against the tolerance they suspected was at the heart of moral relativism. Objective moral truth is a truly dangerous idea. Every moral fanatic the world has ever known has subscribed to it and it is a doctrine which could justify the worst excesses of violence humans are capable of. The view of morality and of moral education suggested in this chapter avoids all talk of values being relative and of objective moral truth as well. Instead the emphasis is placed on the ways in which human beings search for moral meaning and make sense of their moral obligations to one another and how, given some understanding of this, educators – who are not just teachers, but can be found in the family, the community, in the work place, in public life – can help people to a deeper moral understanding of their own being and of the needs of others.

The core of that understanding is that morality is inseparable from the ways in which people live and are valued and experience one another: morality cannot be separated off from everyday human social conduct. It is not a reality set apart to which only the intellectually privileged – the moral philosophers or theologians – or the good – the churchgoers, social workers, doctors and lawyers or teachers – have real access. It cannot be bracketed off as something separate from the main 'subjects' of education or from the ways in which people are valued and defined in the community, the workplace or in society. Above all it is not a static system of rules or codified values but a framework of meaning which develops in response to new and unforeseen circumstances in the lives of human beings. As they struggle to make sense of their changing experiences and face the new dilemmas of their lives, people have to learn the nature of their moral obligations with few direct guides from the past and certainly without adequate information about the consequences of what they choose to do.

Contemporary Moral Discourse

Britain is in the throes of one of its recurring moral panics. The Archbishop of Canterbury, writing in *The Times* (10 April, 1997) described British society as 'morally reticent, even inarticulate ... a society disfigured by widespread moral confusion and false theories of privatised morality'. His solution is to teach morality in schools and to urge particularly strong moral support for the institution of marriage. He welcomes in particular the report mentioned above by SCAA as an important attempt to describe the shared values of our society.

High crime levels, the unacceptable behaviour of the young, political sleaze, the rise in the number of single parent families, the AIDS epidemic, abortion, rising divorce rates all hit the headlines as evidence of moral decline. Candidates to take the blame for it all include the failure of the Church to provide a moral lead to society, the collapse of family life, inadequate moral education in schools, a loss of respect for authority and moral relativism itself. The philosophers compound the problem. Alasdair MacIntyre noted (1981) that people in modern societies have lost the capacity for moral discourse. And those contemporary writers intrigued by the social, cultural and intellectual shifts they characterise as 'post-modernism', which is a generalised loss of faith in all the old certainties – in politics, culture, the arts, in history and morality – detect a moral order to modernity which is diverse to the point of being fragmented and contra-dictory (Bauman, 1993).

In Bauman's analysis, the collapse of older forms of moral discourse does not mean that modern society has become in some way less moral. It means that morality has to find a new grounding. Human beings, he believes, are neither fundamentally good nor fundamentally bad. They are ambivalent. There are no moral guidebooks they can buy but they are capable of acting morally towards one another. The real challenge is to work out the condi-tions under which they would seek to do so.

It could be claimed – indeed, it has been, by Martin Jacques (*The Guardian*, 9 November, 1996) – that far from living in a state of moral decline, 'we now live in a far more demanding moral climate ... Our moral repertoire has expanded enormously. We are now far more morally aware.' Nevertheless, the MORI polls indicate a widespread feeling among the general public of moral decline and a yearning for some way to assert that there are core values by which people should live. How such a framework of agreed values could be arrived at is, of course, to most people, a puzzle. A secular society will not turn to God for the solution of the problem. No one trusts politicians. So what is the solution?

The answer, I believe, can only be found if we re-frame the question and explore critically, in a new kind of dialogue with others, the ways in which moral understanding is constructed, how moral choices are socially situated and how, through time, the relationships between structures in society of power, opportunity, resources and need are articulated and re-defined. People do not have to work out their moral choices from first principles each time they act. What they do in any given situation is something deeply rooted in how they have grown up, how they themselves have been valued as human beings and in the depth and quality of their own moral under-standing. The social circumstances of people's lives are therefore crucial elements of their moral action.

There are no universal moral codes, no absolute values, no objective moral truths. There are social conventions, prevailing views about right and wrong, personal beliefs, commitments and obligations which reflect the values of social groups. Within these we have our capacity to discuss our moral choices, to understand the settings in which we make them and our differing abilities to judge and assess the implications of the choices we and others have made. There is no certainty at the end of this road but there is also no relativism either. What there is is heightened moral awareness, deeper moral sentiment and a strengthened disposition on the part of moral agents to choose the right course of action.

Morality has to be lived and experienced: this is the way in which it is learned. Moral learning is inseparable from how a society is organised and the kinds of values which are promoted by it. Alan Wolfe (1989), in his criticism of both market morality and the moral emptiness of modern social science, has made this point powerfully. He writes (p. 233): 'Moral obligation is a learned practice. If we do not exercise our capacities to act as moral agents, they will atrophy and we will lose them.'

Moral Understanding and Moral Sentiment

Morality comes into view when choices have to be made: to steal something or not, to seek an abortion or not, to be tolerant of opinions different to one's own or not; to meet maintenance payments for a child or not; to put an elderly person in a home or not. Moral thought and action comes into being when people struggle with those decisions. How do they comprehend the choices before them? How do they justify the decisions they make? From where do people acquire the values, moral reasoning and obligations which govern their decisions and actions? How far is moral choice governed by the logic of the situations in which people find themselves? Are some people put in situations where they cannot act morally? Are some situations necessarily contradictory from a moral point of view?

The answer, which is highly relevant to how we understand what is required of moral education, is to acknowledge that there are many situations in which it is simply not clear to people what the right course of action should be. When relationships break up, the balance between self-interest, the needs of children and those of the other partner are very difficult to reconcile. When decisions have to be made to take vulnerable children into care it is virtually impossible to balance the needs of children with those of their parents. If personal promotion at work meant disloyalty towards colleagues, what choices should people make: to place loyalty over personal ambition? How far, in the interests of the smooth running of an organisation, or a family for that matter, is it necessary to tell white lies or to hold back information or to deceive people? What moral justification is there for placing efficiency or expediency above the value of respecting the integrity of other people?

To act morally is hard. It requires a rational justification for the choices one must make within a coherent system of precepts. It presupposes both an understanding of the self and of the Other. Moral action needs sympathy, integrity, knowledge and sometimes sacrifice. It requires the sublimation of self-interest. The relationship between values needs to be thought through. Loyalty, for example, may be considered one of the virtues. It would not be right, however, to allow the value of loyalty to prevent someone from acting justly or with fairness to others. In the process of resolving these questions, people learn about morality. Their choices lead them to particular forms of moral understanding and, therefore, to a view of themselves as moral agents.

In the exercise of that choice, some people become criminals and con men; the practice of deceit for some becomes a high art. We need to know how people come to justify their moral failures as well. What do unfaithful partners say about their behaviour? How do people justify dishonesty? How do managers come to justify taking away the livelihood of their employees through redundancy? How do they use moral language and how did they learn it? What frameworks of meaning do they depend upon? Religion? Politics? Moral Philosophy? How *do* people account for their moral actions? Or is it the case that there are no frameworks, that moral action is situational, that it is pragmatic, conjured up and justified at the point when it is needed and so is provisional and always capable of change?

These are largely empirical questions about which we have few reliable empirical answers. We can at least, however, clarify what kinds of information we need. To act morally requires moral understanding. But that is not enough. A Nazi could be steeped in a knowledge of moral philosophy but decide to act in conscious rejection of all civilised values. Indeed, as Philip Selznick noted, drawing on Hannah Arendt's account of the Eichmann trial in which this Nazi official – Hitler's organiser of the Final Solution – was tried and hanged for crimes against humanity, this is precisely what happened. Adolf Eichmann claimed explicitly that 'he had lived his whole life according to Kant's moral precepts, and especially according to a Kantian definition of duty' (Selznick, 1994, p. 177).

Understanding is therefore not enough. There has to be moral sentiment, sympathy towards and concern for the needs of others together with a strong inner conviction of an obligation to meet those needs. Even this would be insufficient if there was no opportunity to act to do something about it. This is where the situations of moral choice come into view.

In some situations people are positively enabled and encouraged to think about the morality of their choices and to act within their morally grounded convictions. If the situation is about the care of sick relatives or the urgent business of giving help to an accident victim or of giving support to a neighbour, friend or colleague in distress, all but the pathologically self-interested will be clear about the morality of what they must do. Meeting one's moral obligations in such contexts is a relatively straightforward matter, something either born of a deep sense of the rightness of certain actions or called up in a compelling way by the needs of others. Vaclav Havel (1991) has argued that in the first case, i.e. where choices are based on a deep sense of the rightness of the action, people act from a profound, if unarticulated, sense of their 'interexistentiality' – their sense of the fundamental personal reality of the 'I-You' relationship. In respect of the second, Zygmunt Bauman (1995) has suggested that concern for the 'Other' is in some way 'primal'. But it is always ambivalent for no one can know where that responsibility ends or what the consequences are for themselves of meeting or not meeting it.

Nevertheless, this primal concern which is fundamental to our humanity is both fragile – for it can be and is being eroded in modern societies by the market, by business, by political failures and promises to engineer well-being for all citizens – and the basis of all moral hope. The twentieth century has provided too many examples of how, in the interests of political ideology, hate can be harnessed to political ends. Modernity itself, however, has shown how morality can be confined to narrow spheres of life, for example the family, so that other areas – notably the market place or the world of commercial, industrial or political bureaucracy – can become spaces in which people can act with ethical indifference. Philip Selznick has described this process as 'segmental participation' (1994, p. 184). He believes it weakens the sense of personal responsibility that people have towards one another because it insulates large areas of humanity from moral concern.

Bauman (1995, p.261) describes this as a process of *adiaphorization*, a process of exempting personal decisions in certain realms of life from moral evaluation. Bauman's own concern with morality, as someone with a Polish Jewish background, reflects a lifelong attempt to understand the Holocaust. He argues movingly that the further nurturing of the primal moral sense of people, combined with the development of communities in which people are valued and involved, provides the only moral hope for the future and a way of avoiding all the pitfalls of moral relativism on the one hand and the dangers of *adiaphorization* on the other.

This is a powerful argument but it begs the question of where people acquire their 'primal' moral outlook from. A conventional answer is that it derives from their upbringing in the family and the home. Certainly, when questioned, people report their parents as the most important moral role models in their lives. A Guardian/ICM poll found that 88% of respondents (from a national random sample of 1,202 adults) cited their parents as the role models they would wish everyone to follow (*The Guardian*, 7 November, 1996). Educators, though not alone in this view, clearly feel that schools too are crucial in forming the moral outlook of pupils.

From the perspective of adults, this view of the matter can be described as the absorption model of morality: it is something which seeps in as we grow up. Close inspection reveals, however, that in the absence of any coherently grounded morality people fall back on conventional narratives as a way of making sense of their own moral outlook. 'I learned the difference between right and wrong from my parents' is a commonly encountered interpretation. From it flows the view that the moral struggle in our society between Right and Wrong, Good and Evil, must be fought first in the family and then in the school. The argument slides easily on: the moral failures of people – of those who rape, commit crime, steal, deceive others or kill, as well as those who neglect children, ignore marriage vows, or act unreliably – are the outcome of failure in the family or the school. Once the argument has reached this point the necessary action becomes clear: protect family values, strengthen the moral dimension of the curriculum and promote zero-tolerance methods of policing combined with swift and hard punishment.

In social science there is another, equally limited model of moral development: the unfolding flower model or the stages model. With roots in the psychology of Piaget and developed through the work of Lawrence Kohlberg (1984), this asserts that, as they grow up, people pass through various stages of moral-cognitive development. There has been much debate about this and particularly over whether Kohlberg's model is flawed because it is dominated by male notions of moral values and sentiments (see Gilligan, 1993). The real flaw is that the approach is too psychological, too individualistic and underestimates the dilemmas, ambiguities and contingent social character of moral choice in changing societies and the diversity of human experience and social placement which informs moral action.

The prevailing narratives about the sources of morality differ between different groups of people and reflect the social contours of class, gender and generation. At both ends of the social spectrum the narratives become dogmatic with all grasp of the complexities of moral obligation and choice reduced to simple moral axioms devoid of contradiction or doubt. At the extremes of the moral discourse of our society we discover people with the moral understanding of sharks, people whose moral sensibility is corrupted by power and arrogance or by ignorance and greed. They are rare. Far more typical are people who consider themselves to be perfectly normal and reasonably good and who always try to do the right thing. No-one, of course, can always do that. Everyone of us makes the wrong decisions; none of us can fully anticipate all the moral consequences of what we do. It is because of this that it is often asserted that strict moral order has to be maintained and clear values instilled in people just to mitigate the inevitable consequences of human fallibility.

This, of course, is the moral agenda of the political and religious Right. It rests ultimately on the view that human nature is deeply flawed, either by sin or self-interest (though self-interest has been given a new moral legitimacy by the New Right), and can only be regulated by strong support for strict moral codes and by an insistence on the importance of moral absolutes. The socialist/liberal/radical tradition has grounded moral hope in the possibility of social and political change, believing that, if the social circumstances of their lives were better, people themselves would become better. The challenge was to specify what those circumstances should be.

Post-Enlightenment political thought in the radical tradition emphasised the importance of liberty and, later, of democracy. The socialist tributaries to this current of thought added justice, equality and fraternity as the principles to guide the development of the good society. The presumption was that as the weight of exploitation and brutalisation was lifted, human beings would flourish in solidarity with one another. It was Emile Durkheim, the French sociologist, who noted that changes in economic circumstances alone were insufficient to bring about a renewed moral order of society. What was needed was a transformation in the ways in which human beings understood their mutual interdependence. In his view, morality depended on a strong 'collective conscience' which was only possible with the right kind of education and with social and economic policies which promoted a sense of justice and social solidarity.

It was never really an explicit proposition except, perhaps, in the work of Durkheim, but there was always a central assumption in this tradition of social and political thought: people become what they are through the ways in which they participate in society. It is through social participation that people learn about themselves, formulate their personal hopes, understand their obligations to others and imagine alternatives to present-day social arrangements. Sometimes, the learning involved is explicit and intentional. Schools, churches, political parties and voluntary groups have been organised to transmit and nurture the value orientations they consider at the heart of morality. Most often it happens by default. People are taught how to value themselves and others through the ways in which they themselves are treated and expected to participate in the institutions which shape their lives.

The history of the twentieth century has shown that the older versions of liberty were too anaemic and too vulnerable. In the politics of mass society people have been persuaded to sanction genocide. The idea of the sovereign individual acting with moral responsibility has been too easily reduced to the values of the market-place where self-interest takes priority over all other considerations. Bureaucratic work organisations have stripped away the responsibility employees might have for one another by delegating it to managers, limiting the responsibilities of employees to the demands of their own special roles. Caring for the welfare of their colleagues at work is not part of their job description. Thus the world of work has been stripped of its moral content. Efforts in the realm of 'business ethics' to foster strong moral obligations in the work-place invariably run the risk of being undermined by the impersonal logic of the market which privileges the interest of shareholders over those of other stake-holders. The bureaucratic organisation of the modern state means that the responsibility people might feel for one another is transferred to an impersonal agency which organises tax transfers between citizens. In Michael Ignatieff's (1984) striking phrase, it is not a system which encourages people to appreciate and feel responsible for 'the needs of strangers'.

Reduced to the private realm of family life or the dictates of individual conscience, moral obligation becomes a very fragile flower. It requires much stronger support within a whole way of life and an enriched notion of what it means to be a member of society. Such an enriched view, which has to be anchored in the ways in which people view both themselves and other people, is not something to be confined to the moral education of the young. It has to be built into the social institutions of society as a whole, into the jobs people are required to do and into the ways in which people are treated when they become, as we all do, dependent on others. In a secure and loving family, people will grow up feeling valued and will acquire through that a capacity to value others. In a good school, pupils will feel they are valued as ends in themselves and through participation in the collective life of the school learn to take on responsibility and meet their obligations to others. Jobs which require trust, responsibility, truthfulness and honesty as a condition of their performance, will nurture these qualities in the people who do them. Communities which engage their members as citizens and neighbours and value the contribution they make to the common good are likely to promote values like considerateness, tolerance, caring and collective responsibility. The responsibility to promote such values rests, too, with civic leaders, trades unionists, employers and the professions. It is not an abstract responsibility that is required of them. It is a concrete requirement to help build the institutions and working practices to sustain the values which enable people to take part responsibly in the decisions which affect their lives and those of their colleagues, neighbours and fellow citizens.

The opposite of these conditions occurs inevitably when social divisions generate exploitation, exclusion or dehumanisation. Under these conditions – and terms like these describe only too well the experience of many people in our society – people are driven into narrow, meaningless worlds and perceive others through the narrow filters of their own limited experience and shallow personal hopes. It is not a matter of whether people are rich or poor. It is about the frameworks of meaning – or, as Vaclav Havel has noted, of the opposite of meaningfulness, absurdity – in which people live their lives. When social relationships become devoid of a purpose and meaning oriented towards the well-being of others, moral sentiment can, as has been argued earlier, atrophy into indifference or apathy

Conclusion
Running throughout this chapter is the claim that morality is part of the warp and weft of society and of social experience. The moral self is

nurtured in social contexts and develops through learning and through being a member of and living within a society and making the moral decisions which are inescapably part of being a sentient human being. Denied that opportunity to reflect upon morality, to engage in what Selznick (1994, p. 36) has called 'moral inquiry', people will not develop an understanding of their moral nature as human beings. Only through changes in the organisation of work and community can people secure the opportunity of engaging in moral dialogue with each other. Neither a tradition-bound model of moral discourse nor the unfolding flower model of moral development is adequate. Only through an enriched notion of citizenship which embraces all the domains – family, education, work, community – in which people interact with one another, can moral understanding, sentiment and development be achieved.

If these general lines of approach to the nature of moral discourse in societies like ours have validity, it becomes very clear that pontifical assertions about moral absolutes or brave efforts to root morality and moral education in the important but limited domain of family life are an inadequate and ultimately pessimistic response to the particular moral crises of our times. There is greater moral hope in a different approach, one which stresses the fundamental moral nature of all human action and, through that, understands that morality – which is always ambiguous – must be constantly discussed and debated so as to be understood. It is a process of learning throughout a lifetime. People require support and help to do so and modern societies and cultures must be capable of change in order to respond to what people have come to know. As for moral education in schools, the best that must be done is so to arrange the organisation of schools that all children can be respected as citizens and can be engaged directly in dialogue about how their schools should be managed and about what kinds of values they should nurture. The debate must, however, go further, to enable children – and, in the case of colleges and universities, young people – to consider carefully the moral dilemmas of adulthood in the kind of society in which they live. Educators must help children and young people to acquire the skills to engage in such discussions. The school cannot be the model for society: society must be the model for the school, but only if its values stand the test of a rigorous moral scrutiny.

Acknowledgements

I would like to thank Gerald Collier for his careful and helpful criticism of this chapter.

Chapter 9

Judgement Day

Richard Smith

In chapter 16 of Mark Twain's *Huckleberry Finn* Huck is travelling down the Mississippi on a raft with the slave, Jim, whom he has helped to escape from his owner, Miss Watson. The plan is to reach Cairo, where the Mississippi meets the Ohio, to sell the raft and take a steamboat up the Ohio to the free States where Jim will no longer have the status of a slave. It is night, and Jim jumps with excitement every time he thinks he sees the lights of Cairo. Huck's conscience begins to worry him. Isn't Jim Miss Watson's property? Isn't Huck aiding and abetting a theft, and a theft moreover from someone who tried to be good to Huck 'every way she knowed how'? Huck's torment grows as the excited Jim talks about how when he gets to a free State he will work and work to buy his wife, owned by a neighbouring farmer to Miss Watson, out of slavery, 'and then they would both work to buy the two children, and if their master wouldn't sell them, they'd get an Ab'litionist to go and steal them'.

Huck tells us that 'it most froze' him to hear such talk. He knows that there is a rule, indeed a Commandment, against stealing; that Jim is doing wrong, and planning to do more wrong, and that he, Huck, is up to his moral neck in the wrongdoing.

> Here was this nigger which I had as good as helped to run away, coming right out flat-footed and saying he would steal his children – children that belonged to a man I didn't even know; a man that hadn't ever done me no harm.

So Huck resolves to give Jim up to the authorities, and with this decision made his conscience grows easy. He tells Jim he is going to paddle ashore in the canoe to see whether these lights really are the lights of Cairo. Fifty yards off he comes across two men in a skiff. They establish that he belongs to the raft they glimpse in the darkness. Are there any men on it? they ask. One man, replies Huck. Is he white or black? There are runaway slaves in the vicinity, and these men make money by catching them. Huck's resolve weakens: he answers 'He's white.' And when the men decide to check for themselves, Huck tricks them into thinking that the raft carries his father, sick with small-pox. At this the two men back away fast, and float two twenty-dollar gold pieces to Huck on a wooden board. They have consciences too.

What of Huck's conscience? He knows he has done wrong, and puts it down to his upbringing, seeing it as what happens when someone 'don't get *started* right when he's little'. But further reflection leads him to realise that he would feel just as bad if he had stuck to his original resolution to hand Jim over. So Huck decides to give up on the whole business of morality: 'I reckoned I wouldn't bother no more about it, but after this always do whatever came handiest at the time.'

This moving story reminds us of a number of things. First, it reminds us of the variety and complexity of the moral life. It reminds us that as well as moral principles or rules there are the demands of the kind of fellow-feeling that Huck succumbs to; that there is what the welfare of others, in general or in any particular case, requires us to do; that we naturally care, and feel that we ought to care, for those close to us. The moral life contains other elements still. For example, what we understand as 'the good life for humankind', involving the fulfilment of such potential as we may have and the exercise of our higher capacities, makes demands that seem to have moral force in that it would surely be *wrong* to waste our talents. Then too we are increasingly willing to identify the environment, or 'the planet', as the source of moral claims that cannot simply be explained in terms of the rights of other people, alive or still to be born, or of animals or trees and wildernesses. The elements of the moral life can conflict and often do, which is why Huckleberry Finn's conscience troubles him, why life presents us endlessly with moral problems and dilemmas, and why it is hard to be absolute about even the soundest moral principles.

The story also reminds us that societies and cultures often differ in the extent to which they value or foreground the various elements of morality. Twain's novel can be read as a dramatisation of the values of 'liberty, equality and fraternity' which inspired the American Revolution as much as the French one. Where the northern European, Kantian or Protestant, traditions had tended to emphasise somewhat austere moral principles it was natural for societies that were rejecting existing forms of patriarchy to seek moral salvation in fraternity or fellow-feeling. A late twentieth-century multicultural society, unsurprisingly, tends to see more value in tolerance than a beleaguered, militaristic one such as ancient Sparta. A society which increasingly accords women equal status to men is likely to see moral worth in *caring*; a society which for all kinds of complicated socio-economic reasons is dominated by a culture of individualism will express its moral values in terms of 'rights' more than a society where a genuinely communitarian ethos prevails.

Through this historical perspective we can see that morality is not something wholly abstract and independent of particular societies and their practices. It is brought into being to do certain jobs: to counteract our destructive tendency to selfishness, for example, and to repair our limited capacity for experiencing the kind of human sympathy that Huck feels towards Jim. (Huck's own capacity is limited: it does not extend very far in the direction of the Widow Douglas or Miss Watson.) This is not to make out a case for 'relativism' on the grounds that moral values are local and temporary phenomena, still less that they are *merely* so. For one thing, since human nature and fundamental human needs stay much the same over time it is easy to exaggerate the extent to which the elements of morality change. We continue to admire courage, for instance, since it is a virtue much needed in any world we are likely to inhabit, even if at one time our paradigm is the courage of the buccaneer (Drake, Raleigh, Grenville and Howard were the names of the 'houses' in my primary school) and at another the courage of the single mother heroically struggling to make a good life for herself and her children. For another, noting that morality arises as a response to our needs as a species and as members of particular societies should lead us to observe that we have a continual duty to scrutinise the adequacy of the moral ideas that operate in our own time and place. We rightly find it appalling that many ordinary Germans went along with the idea that non-Aryans were sub-human; we find it disturbing that many of our forefathers uncritically accepted it as a given truth that women were intrinsically inferior. Similarly we want youngsters to look beyond the values of their peer-group and see that while virtues such as loyalty are to be prized there are other values, such as repudiating outright criminality, that loyalty may come into conflict with. Here the job that moral thinking does is to protect us from complacency, the lazy sophism of 'we all have the values of the culture we grow up in, so I don't have any choice.'

Just as we shall make no sense of morality, however, while we are in the grip of the idea that 'values all come down to personal opinion' (since this is precisely to deny the possibility of morality), so too our understanding of morality will not advance beyond the primitive while we are haunted by the search for 'absolutes'. It may well be true, as Talbot and Tate insist in their chapter, that we value justice and freedom absolutely. Yet this is no more than to insist on the unavoidability of the institution of morality itself: to insist that a world recognisably like our own cannot be conceived in non-moral terms. Important though this point is, it gives us no guidance on what to do when moral values – justice and freedom, for example – conflict, as when considerations of what is *fair* may lead us to limit a talented child's freedom to win all the prizes in open competition. It does not in itself help with those difficult cases where we have to decide whether justice, say, involves distribution equally, according to need or according to merit. And it is among cases like this that all of us, children included, live the greater part of our moral lives: witness any group of five year-olds trying to decide what constitutes equitable access to the more popular toys.

It is a very mixed benefit to children to emphasise for them the 'absolute' dimension of morality, since they are usually only too ready to see things in term of moral blacks and whites:

> 'Jason has broken our rule which says we walk down the corridor. What should we do?'

> 'Make him lose his playtime for a week, Miss!'

> 'On the other hand, he was running after Melanie to tell her she'd dropped her scarf.'

> 'But he was running, Miss, he should lose his playtimes – '

> ' – for a month, Miss!'

> ' – for the rest of the term!'

Here attachment to the absolute is a sign of the under-developed sense of morality that fails to see the importance of the circumstances of the particular case.

Aristotle (*Nicomachean Ethics* I.3) observed that the reasonable person looks only for as much exactness as the subject-matter admits. Three plus three makes six, irrespective of what things you are counting; Ohm's Law operates without regard for mitigating factors such as the age of the electrician who connects up the circuit. Moral principles, on the other hand, as Aristotle also noted (*ibid.*), operate 'for the most part'. Killing is wrong, but not, perhaps, if it is the only way to stop a mass-murderer. You should tell the truth, but there are times when a lie is not merely permissible but preferable ('You're looking really well'), generally when the moral principle of truth-telling is trumped by that other major element of the moral life, regard for the welfare of others. It is not a weakness of moral principles that they apply 'for the most part' and cannot be used in the form of rigid algorithms, any more that it is a weakness of the principles of literary criticism that George Eliot cannot be *conclusively* proved to be a finer novelist than Barbara Cartland. It simply is the nature of moral principles that they are like this; and there is a case for saying that in this consists their peculiar and disturbing force – that it is in this that they are uniquely fitted to the contingency of human life (see Martha Nussbaum, 1986).

From here we can see how the notion of moral *judgement* is of fundamental importance. We use moral judgement when we weigh up a situation and seek to bring to it a suitable balance of the moral elements – principles, certainly, but also concern for particular others, fellow-feeling, the attempt to calculate benefits against harm, and so on – which is what Huckleberry Finn appears to do instinctively in his moral dilemma. To some, talk of 'judgement' has connotations of judgementalism, of 'sitting in judgement' (Matthew, 11. 24: 'But I say unto you, That it shall be more tolerable for the land of Sodom in the day of judgement, than for thee'). On the contrary, however, emphasis on the importance of moral judgement foregrounds the need for a responsiveness to people and to individual cases which is wholly at odds with rushing to conclusions about them. An example may make this clearer.

A not uncommon quandary for parents occurs when they find evidence of cannabis use in a teenager's bedroom. A friend of a friend described to me his reactions to just this discovery. His first thought was that the use of cannabis is illegal, and moreover constitutes 'drug taking', which as a general idea he finds abhorrent. Before rushing to judgement and confronting his daughter, however, he paused to reflect. Was there evidence of other drug use, or any suggestion that the girl was dealing in drugs? That she was suffering from taking cannabis, for example in the deterioration of her schoolwork, or becoming anti-social? He wondered whether he ought to regard occasional cannabis use – if this was what had been going on – by the norms of his daughter's generation, and so as little more cause for concern than his own occasional illicit cigarette at the same age. What was the issue here anyway: was it one of legality, addiction, of potential harm to his daughter, or was it a case of an incipient lifestyle from which he wanted to discourage her on the grounds that there are richer and more fulfilling ways to live a life? The example shows how much turns on the circumstances of the particular case, and on which balance of the moral elements we bring to bear on it.

The conclusion to this man's exercise of his moral (and prudential, it must be added) judgement was as follows. First of all, he felt there was an issue here that must not be ducked. He told his daughter he felt there was a crucial distinction between occasional, 'recreational' use of cannabis and regular use amounting to dependency, let alone the use of more dangerous drugs. He encouraged her to take up again some of her old interests that she seemed to have dropped, such as swimming and playing the piano. He acknowledged the breach of privacy of the girl's bedroom that had occurred, but was prepared to justify it on the grounds of his concern for her. And he was prepared to acknowledge the force of the criticism that she made in return: 'how is this different from the amount of drink *you* put away?' In all this he was sensitive to the fact that in a sense parents are not meant to 'win' conflicts like these: they are in part ways in which young people establish that they hold their values separately, even if they often turn out to be very similar values, for better or worse. He was able to express his points in the form: 'this is so, isn't it?' – registering the force of what he believed, and the reasons for it, while opening up room for disagreement and dialogue (the diminishing quantity and quality of which between himself and his daughter he was inclined to believe was a significant issue).

Now this is a long way from judgementalism. It bears some interesting parallels with the way in which we form literary judgements: trying to read a text carefully and sensitively in its own terms, not rushing to form a conclusion prematurely, testing our own interpretations against others' (subjectivists will avoid this on the grounds that 'it's all a matter of opinion', refusing to believe that the judgement of an experienced and careful reader may be sharper than that of the occasional consumer of 'airport fiction'; absolutists will believe that there must be a once-and-for-all answer somewhere – an idea even odder in literary than in moral judgement). The literary critic F. R. Leavis, who more than most insisted on the essentially *moral* role of literature, used to say that literary appraisal characteristically took the form of asking 'It is so, isn't it?' Here the first 'is' can be emphasised appropriately to the importance of what is at stake, while the voice must rise on the final 'it' to reflect the idea that any literary judgement, like any moral one, can be re-visited and re-appraised. Our views of, say, Restoration drama change from generation to generation, as do our moral views – of the moral standing of animals, for instance. This does not make them 'relative' in any pernicious sense.

Reading and sharing literature, or stories more generally, may be one of the best ways we have of teaching children to make moral judgements as well as literary ones, and of teaching them the characteristic way such judgements are formed and held. From the character of Toad in *The Wind in the Willows* (loveable rogue? bombastic coward?) to that of Mary Crawford in *Mansfield Park* ('Good fun for a one-night stand', said Mr Browne, my sixth-form teacher, 'but you wouldn't *marry* her'; he knew that moral education may need to shock from time to time) literature and its people can be revisited with growing understanding, and they become the vehicles of that understanding (compare A. S. Byatt, quoted above, p. 45-46). The same is true for myths and legends. As we grow older the Odysseus we encountered as children comes to seem a more ambivalent and less simply heroic figure, just as on a more sophisticated level Jane Austen's Mr Bennett (*Pride and Prejudice*) appears more irresponsible and less attractively ironic 'That's right, isn't it?'. In such ways our moral as well as our literary vision expands. We become able to see more of the world and to see it, as it seems to us, more accurately and less partially.

In some respects the opportunities to learn judgement are now rarer than they were. The conditions of modern life – so many more cars on the roads, and the rare but well-publicised child murders – mean that adults become reluctant to let children learn from their own mistakes as they painfully acquire street-wisdom. Making mistakes in *education* will in any case be anathematised as schools turn themselves into 'totally effective' institutions, 'high reliability organisations' (Reynolds, 1995) for whom it is as unacceptable to get it right only 99% of the time as it would be for an airline to have one in every hundred of its planes crash: a curious idea which, if (impossibly) it could be implemented, would succeed in eliminating choice and the risk of making the wrong choice, and so would destroy the moral dimension of schooling altogether. Furthermore the stories and the literature which I have argued are a fine training-ground for moral judgement are in decline in the classroom and threatening to disappear. Story-time for six year-olds has no obvious outcomes and looks less likely to help the school climb the league-table than some solid work on spelling, and there is a tendency for literature to be replaced, in English as a curriculum subject, by the acquisition of linguistic skills supposed to increase the children's chances of getting jobs and (perhaps *or*) filling in forms correctly. Such literature as does escape the purge may do so largely in virtue of its being part of 'our heritage' – a universal 'entitlement' to compulsory Shakespeare or some such muddle – with the implication that it is to be treated with awe and respect, something like Westminster Abbey, rather than read critically with all the possibilities for personal growth which that entails.

The *political* conditions of the last twenty years or so have marginalised the role of judgement as effectively as the educational ones. Ian (now Lord) Gilmour remarks on this in his critique of the 'Thatcher years', *Dancing With Dogma* (1992, p. 208 f.). The belief grew that there are on the one hand hard facts, such as those of science and perhaps the invincible laws of economics, and on the other there is personal taste or choice – Essex Man may spend his weekends polishing his Ford Sierra or going to the supermarket, it's up to him for this is a free society – while everything else can be, and *ought* to be, left in the hands of 'the market'. *Here there is no room left for judgement.* The professionals who had once been seen as, precisely, those who had acquired a trained and informed judgement in their special areas of expertise were now routinely denigrated as the self-serving defenders of their own 'producer interests'. Who were teachers to say that children ought to be given an anti-racist education, or that it was as important to respect difference in the classroom as it was to learn the date of the Battle of Waterloo? Power passed to consumers, who were fortified with charters of their rights and supplied with school league-tables to inform their choices, in a perfect illustration of the notion that hard facts and choice together constitute all that you need before you act.

Meanwhile the scope for the exercise of teachers' professional judgement, even for those who still felt the inclination to use it, was becoming steadily eroded. First, of course, the National Curriculum told them *what* to teach and then, increasingly, government ministers and advisers, Chief Inspectors of Schools and Sunday journalists told them *how* to teach it: didactically and from the front of the class, in a way that could be acclaimed as 'traditional' (another aspect of our national heritage, perhaps). Often this was described as an attempt to 'open up debate'. But care was taken to demonise anyone whose judgement might lead them to join the debate on the other side, to resist the new orthodoxy and to object to the way it was being imposed. Academic educationists and local authority advisers were singled out as the cause of the rot; the contemptuous label 'progressive' could be attached to those whom it was difficult to categorise and dismiss on any other grounds. The booming economies of the Pacific Rim, whose classrooms were held up as paradigms of good practice, were used as bugbears to frighten away the last tendencies to engage in rational argument and debate about education. These were not conditions to allow personal and professional judgement to flourish. Its exercise was replaced by adherence to the programmes of study, guidelines and policy statements that the new managerialism and centralised bureaucracy had spawned.

In all this there seemed to be a *fear* of the use of judgement, a terror that if teachers were allowed to use their own judgement they would promptly abandon maths lessons for peace education, anti-racism and sessions designed to promote homosexuality. Much, of course, has been made of the occasions when the judgement of teachers and other educationists left itself open to question: a headteacher who complained that *Romeo and Juliet* celebrated heterosexuality too exclusively, or a local education authority adviser who found 'creativity' in a pupil's essay where few others could see anything but mis-spellings and chaotic grammar ('English as she is tort', *The Guardian,* 9 October 1992). But to limit, or to eliminate, the scope for judgement on the strength of a handful of such cases makes no more sense than preventing children from playing in the park on the grounds than every now and then one of them falls over and grazes its knee (in both cases it is arguable that the solution lies in having *more* opportunities for practising judgement, not less).

If we are to re-instate moral judgement as a crucial element of the moral life then it is important that we understand what it consists of. Its key features are attentiveness, a kind of self-awareness, flexibility and the right use of experience. *Attentiveness*, first, is displayed when a teacher is alert to the myriad details that lead her to interpret this situation as one where a pupil needs to be challenged and 'stretched' and that situation – which to an outsider may look remarkably similar – as one where a pupil needs encouragement and the reassurance of a degree of repetition. In the classroom, as in the home, everything is in the detail: the indefinable set of circumstances which tell us that now is not the time to be overly critical of the last homework assignment or, in the home, that questions about the outcome of the latest test are best left until later. These, it must be noted, are *moral* matters; education is thoroughly suffused with moral matters, which do not arise solely on the occasions when we sit down to discuss moral dilemmas about under-age drinking or abortion. To fail to see that a pupil is bored and in need of stimulus, or, in the home rather than the school, to jump in with questions when your own child is tired and ragged, is (morally) insensitive, if understandable. To bring your own anxiety to such situations, and to respond principally in the light of your own needs and vulnerabilities, is, while natural, to fail to do full justice – a moral matter – to what the situation requires.

From this follows the importance of *self-awareness*. Doing our best by other people requires that we have some sense of our own strengths and weaknesses. We need to know, for instance, when we are tired and liable to respond tetchily, so that we can take those few vital extra seconds before we reply to the question that we at first see as provocative, a 'wind up'. We need to reflect on both the critical incidents and the casual business of the day: were we too quick to condemn, or on the other hand too slow to register our disapprobation? Is the child we have readily categorised as tiresome and juvenile rather to be thought of as a lively, spontaneous ten year-old? Should we really dismiss our colleagues as insular and unsupportive, or ought we to be more aware that they too suffer from stress and the sense that their efforts are unregarded? In this way self-awareness acts as a check on self-interest and self-regard.

In being willing to revisit and revise our judgement we display appropriate *flexibility*. Rather than issue blanket condemnations of, say, cheating, we take the trouble to distinguish the behaviour of the child who has casually plundered the work of his peers from that of the child who has worked collaboratively, in good faith, where collaborative work was inappropriate. Such flexibility on the part of teacher or parent is profoundly educative for the child, who thus comes to realise that the world is a morally complex place that can be interpreted in various lights and is seldom reducible to moral black-and-white. The flexibility of moral judgement consists in the moulding of our apprehension to the contours of what we apprehend. Aristotle (*Nicomachean Ethics* v. 10) used a vivid image to make this feature of judgement memorable: the builders of the island of Lesbos, who used a malleable lead ruler in making a certain sort of moulding. 'The rule adapts itself to the shape of the stone and is not rigid, and so too the decree is adapted to the facts' (Ross's 1969 translation; we might say, 'the judgement is adapted to the circumstances').

Lastly, good moral judgement involves *reflection on experience*. We learn to distinguish the morally relevant features of situations, perceiving those which are and those which are not similar to previous ones. We learn to revisit with honest scrutiny areas of our own past that are not always comfortable to recall. The self-deceiver, the wishful thinker and the denier display poor moral judgement, since they cannot look on their experience with an unclouded eye, if they can look on it at all. They may well prefer the crutch of rigid principles which save them having to confront the often confusing fluidity of reality. The proper use of experience also involves noticing the propensity of the present and the future to be unlike the past, and a preparedness to be open to the uniqueness of events. Experience teaches us not to rely on experience over-much. Here the features of moral judgement – attentiveness, self-awareness, flexibility and the use of experience – can be seen working in complex interrelation.

Moral judgement seems to share the same structure as practical judgement more generally: practical judgement, to put it the other way round, has a moral side that cannot be separated out. That is why the moral dimension of our lives cannot be treated as some sort of optional extra, to be bolted back onto a morally indifferent world whenever we are shocked to notice how badly the children are behaving. We are all the time negotiating the world and our encounters with other people with the help of concepts that are irreducibly moral. We see another person in one light as solid and dependable and in another as dull and conventional; as deeply reflective or alternatively as self-indulgent; as 'good fun' or as light-weight and too exuberant; as forbearing or as down-trodden. These are moral concepts, containing approbation or disapprobation. We have a responsibility to see other people accurately, since from our view of them will follow the way we treat them. And we have a further responsibility to acquire the most responsive set of concepts in this area. Someone who can only bring the crudest set of ideas to bear, dividing the world exclusively into 'them and us', for example, or who insists on seeing all women as excessively emotional or all men as nothing but overgrown boys, is allowing themselves to go badly equipped about the world just as surely as if they drove a car with bald tyres, with no spare and dangerously low on oil.

Too much emphasis on moral *principles* obscures this important point. Moral principles (to repeat) have their place among the elements of the moral life, and may have crucial significance from time to time. For example, there is evidence that your chances of survival in a concentration camp were improved if your foreman was a man of iron principle, such as a hard-line communist or a Jehovah's Witness (Benson, 1983, drawing on Bettelheim's book *The Informed Heart*). But exaggeration of the importance of moral principles across the whole range of moral experience acts as a standing invitation not only to conceive moral thinking as a search for the rigid and unvarying guidance of rules, but to see that search, and the use of rules, as something for special occasions only: for when we are confronted with a dilemma, or when we are discussing euthanasia or genetic engineering. It obscures the way that the moral dimension colours the whole of our lives. It encourages us to place morality in a ghetto called moral education, remote from the daily lives and concerns of teachers, parents and children themselves.

Every day is judgement day, and not only those on which we remember to turn our thoughts explicitly to moral matters.

One set of practical conclusions following from this chapter, then, relates to the danger of confining moral education to a self-contained curricular slot. Another set concerns the importance for children of those forms of understanding and experience, in particular the literary, through which we develop our capacity for judgement in general and moral judgement in particular. Perhaps the most important conclusion, however, especially in the present climate, seems to me to do with teachers, parents and other carers rather than directly with children themselves. We cannot expect children to learn moral judgement from adults who are too nervous to exercise it, or who are working in climates of regulation and control where their capacity for judgement is curtailed. The constant tendency to distrust the judgement of teachers in particular and to deny them space to use it needs to be reversed, with a reduction in centralised government control and interference. Other ways of encouraging professional responsibility and monitoring professional standards, such as the institution of a General Teaching Council, might be more effective in this respect, and would be more likely to respect the nature of personal and professional judgement, moral and otherwise.

As a coda, it is worth remarking that re-drawing our picture of the moral life to give moral judgement its due allows us to understand rather better our own responsibilities as adults, parents and teachers. While talk of moral principles risks suggesting a lofty standard which we must reach on pain of the accusation of hypocrisy, recognition of the nature and role of judgement accepts that judgement may be faulty from time to time without moral damnation for its owner (indeed, unless our judgement failed us quite often it is hard to see how we could ever learn anything). We want those around us, including children, to be generally honest, loyal, truthful people, and we want them to have principles which they maintain 'for the most part', using their judgement to make exceptions for good reasons and with regard to all the different elements of the moral life, including our welfare and the welfare of others. Huckleberry Finn's view of these things, in the opening sentences of the novel, is perhaps as judicious as any we can find:

> You don't know about me, without you have read a book by the name of *The Adventures of Tom Sawyer*, but that ain't no matter. That book was made by Mr Mark Twain, and he told the truth, mainly. There was things which he stretched, but mainly he told the truth. That is nothing. I never seen anybody but lied, one time or another ...

Anything more than this, the whole novel seems to tell us, risks being an altogether too artificial and sanctimonious version of morality, and that will have any sane child heading for the hills with Huck Finn.

Chapter 10

Spirituality, Anti-intellectualism, and the End of Civilisation as We Know It

Nigel Blake

Anti-intellectualism in Britain is neither left-wing nor right-wing: it's endemic. By 'anti-intellectualism', I mean a mistrust of canonic standards and practices of intellectual discourse and debate, standards and practices which might stand in the way of personal or sectional convictions. Often this comes down to a dogged cleaving to 'common sense'. However, in the 1970s, anti-intellectualism enjoyed a most paradoxical incarnation in the self-proclaimed Leftism of educational relativism. The paradox was to find an excuse for derogations of objectivity and rigour, dressed in the garb of a supposedly objective and rigorous, but elaborate, specious and hyper-intellectual form of neo-Marxism. In this manifestation, the shakiest feature of Marxism, its theory of ideology, was exacerbated by the importation of ill-understood notions from epistemology and psychology. By this stratagem, neo-Marxists contrived to impugn the standards apposite to their own practice as merely ideological.

So what happened to anti-intellectualism? By some peculiar process I don't pretend to understand, it has re-emerged in the 1990s in the dangerous form of what I shall call for convenience 'conservative spirituality'. (Throughout this essay, I mean 'small 'c' conservative'. Of course, this overlaps with Toryism, all the same.) And herein lies another paradox. To understand this paradox, we need first to grasp the problems with that earlier bout of relativist anti-intellectualism. There are two such problems and they are inter-linked.

Uppermost in people's minds in recent years has been the issue of moral relativism. There is a fear that a shared understanding of right and wrong has been dissipated, and so too, it is inferred, our very care for what really is right and wrong and thus any disposition to behave with decency. But worse, many fear that we have lost our belief in even the possibility of a common framework within which moral disagreements can be credibly addressed. To deny such possibilities of moral debate and objectivity is relativism. Those who refuse to reassert some common framework are taken to be moral relativists and a danger to civilised life.

Underneath the issue of moral relativism, we might find the 1970s legacy of epistemological relativism – relativism in the very sphere of knowledge, the idea that there are no objective facts in life, just different ways of 'seeing things' and no way of choosing between a better and a worse way. (From here it is a short step to inferring that all knowledge is actually mere ideology.) Here there is an apparent guarantee for moral relativism. If we can't even say that we know what's what in the physical world, we have less than no chance in the realm of morals. And yet it is indeed a great scandal of progressive educational thought in the 1970s that it was hijacked by such ill-considered relativist 'dogma', the only word for it.

Reaction against relativism is now well-entrenched. In January 1996, about 200 participants attended the conference sponsored by SCAA, *Education for Adult Life: the spiritual and moral development of young people* – let's call them 'the SCAA 200' (and not confuse them with the 150 members of the National Forum for Values in Education, established after the conference). These were the '[school] governors, parents, youth workers, employers, religious leaders and academics' (SCAA Discussion Papers: No 6, Introduction – all page references are to this document) in whose name we are presented with the solemn nonsense presented in this report.

The national context of that conference mixed elements of farce with tragedy. The farce was that of a failing Conservative government grasping at credibility with the call of 'Back to Basics' – which soon began to seem little more than a cloak for 'Back to my place!' And the pages examined below are worthy of that shabby and silly period in public life.

Yet nonsense though these pages are, the conference which they invoke for their own legitimacy was a conscious and explicit response to a tragic event which crystallised widespread worries about the moral state of contemporary society and of the young in particular. The tragedy was the murder of head teacher Philip Lawrence in the course of an argument outside his own school gates, by a youngster from another school. This murder struck deep in the feelings of the nation. For, as a successful and respected Head working hard in a difficult inner-city area, Philip Lawrence's murder seemed surely a kind of patricide – the killing of a Good Father. More than most murders, this one seemed to point to a frightening emptiness somewhere in our society. Another horrifying event, but not mentioned in the Report, had stoked deep anxieties concerning children, and that was the murder of little James Bulger by two other children. Whatever the inadequacies of the response of the following Report, the SCAA 200 must have had a passionate sense of what they were here for. And charity towards them is appropriate. When looking into the abyss, it's understandable to grasp for a superhuman hand to hold. If what follows is far less charitable to the Report itself, it's because educational responsibility demands something very different from an exploitation of intimate fear.

What they were there for, according to the SCAA agenda, was to 'discover' some moral consensus amongst men and women of good will which could be confidently reasserted in the face of a society on the slide. It seemed to be taken for granted that this was a precondition of any credible programme of moral re-development. And of course, there is much in the Report that one has to agree with. Pap and truisms are like that. 'Those engaged on school-based projects ... appeared to have no difficulty in producing lists of qualities desirable in young people' (p. 10). No, I bet they didn't – agreement on the vague is only too easy and no guarantee of insight or truth. If they had had difficulty, it might have been evidence of serious thinking. The Report is consistently glib.

Yet side by side with the resoundingly obvious in this report is the downright peculiar: stuff one can only credit on the assumption that the Report doesn't actually mean what it says (a possibility I'll return to). For instance, consensus was assumed, arbitrarily, to pertain to something called 'core values'. No-one is reported as having questioned the validity of this ethical novelty, as unfamiliar to Rawls, MacIntyre or Habermas as to Plato, Aristotle or Kant, notwithstanding its provenance in contemporary management theory, the most dubious branch of 'knowledge' in our entire culture ('[They] pointed out that many organisations have developed statements of core values to which all employees can subscribe', p. 10). And no-one explored the very plausible idea that it's much easier to agree on what is right and wrong than it is to agree on why 'this' is right and 'that' is wrong, and that there may be no 'core values' that we share even if we have areas of overlapping moral agreement. (The idea of an 'overlapping consensus', which makes no assumption of shared 'core values', features in the important work of John Rawls.)

As we will immediately see, however, one of the 'core' ideas of the conference was supposedly, if quite remarkably, that morality is linked to, or an extension of, 'the spiritual'. Thus on p. 6 we read: 'There was broad acceptance of the view of spirituality in *Spiritual and Moral Development* – a discussion document republish by SCAA in 1995'; 'Many delegates perceived a close relationship between spirituality and moral development ... Spirituality can be seen as the source of the will to act morally'; and (p.7) '*Delegates agreed* [*sic* – my italics] that 'spiritual and moral development' is important in education'. We are then launched straight into a chapter on moral education as if it followed seamlessly.

Yet in the canon of western thought, as I shall argue, this idea is frankly bizarre: and it is difficult to believe that 200 intelligent people really were at ease in supporting it. So I shall talk below of the SCAA 'consensus', asking the reader to attend to the scare quotes and to wonder whether this consensus is not notional rather than real. The Report is a very subtle piece of writing. (And SCAA has the subtlety not to put a name to it.) It does not claim complete consensus on every point – clearly that would strain credibility. There are plenty of allusions all through to what 'some' people think and to certain differences at least of emphasis. But those differences which are mentioned seem to be portrayed as secondary in importance. And one cannot have any confidence that all disagreements have received the consideration they deserve. 200 serious people just can't have been this foolish.

It is this grounding of consensus in the most radically implausible assumptions possible which this essay deals with. My concern is both with its actual, if unrecognised, undermining of morality and with the object lesson it provides us in the limitations of a managed consensus whose conclusions seem largely to have been pre-empted.

We first glimpse the guiding assumption of the Report obliquely in the comment 'Some questioned the assumption that secularism and relativism have triumphed...' (p.7). Here, relativism is identified as pre-eminent amongst the enemies to be beaten, but moreover it seems that secularism is somehow linked to it. We are not actually told that secularists are relativists or that secularism leads inevitably to relativism. But it seems to this reader that what's really being said is this: the ultimate truths are spiritual truths. So if we are mired in a relativistic cultural decay, only a revived spirituality can save us. And if a spiritual view of life alone can rebut relativism, so a secular view must support relativism, if only by default. An effective revival of moral education must take place within a context of spiritual education, conceived moreover as an explicit antidote to secularism.

The presumptive intellectual rationale for such a view is made more explicit a little later:

> Delegates suggested several causes for the present situation with regard to moral values. These include:
>
> - Dominant intellectual currents. Philosophical approaches since the eighteenth century were broadly seen to have resulted in the triumph of relativism, the desire to tolerate and respect all beliefs and lifestyles, and the belief that education should be value-free. Moral relativism derives from the demise of religion, the assumption that without God there can be no absolutes. (p. 8)

And here's the paradox. The paradox is that the project of redeeming knowledge, education and morality through spirituality in itself undermines, as we see in this quotation, the very traditions in whose name educators have claimed their cultural authority, these past two hundred years. Conservative spirituality repudiates both the social tradition and the intellectual achievements of the Enlightenment Project, whilst claiming, at times, to revive traditional values. Is it then postmodern? No, of course not; rather it is pre-modern, a cultural regression. It is every bit as insidious in education as the relativism and subjectivism of the 1970s; just as likely to corrupt and destroy 'civilisation as we know it' – the culture of rational civility and civic rationality and the integrity of culture itself.

For if there is a mark of the person genuinely committed against relativism, then it's a desire to 'get it right' or at least to try to avoid error; and this intrinsically involves a commitment to rational argument. (Dogmatists repudiate relativism, whilst arguably practising it in their highhanded dismissal of dissent as if it made no contact with 'their' reality.) This intrinsic antithesis between relativism and reason needs emphasising in its own right. In its covertly authoritarian way, the Report sees difference and disagreement as the real problem with relativism. But mere agreement is no guarantee against relativism and disagreement no sign of it. Even, perhaps especially, a national agreement on core values (see the Report, p. 10) can yet be relativist if it isn't established by means of rational debate but by assertion and conformism. A complete moral consensus can indeed be completely relativist (even where appeal is made to 'absolutes' – see below). And conversely, disagreement need not be relativist if it arises in the context of rational argument.

With that in mind, when we are told in the quotation above that the SCAA 200 see modern philosophy 'to have resulted in the triumph of relativism, the desire to tolerate and respect all beliefs and lifestyles, and the belief that education should be value-free', the first question has to be 'Why? Why should an educated group believe anything so ill-informed?' What depths of philosophical ignorance are attributed here to the conference audience? And what does this tell us about the Report? Does it not reveal the author's own casual indifference to distinctions of right and wrong which shows the Report to be no more reliable as a moral guide than the work of any relativist?

For no-one would do philosophy at all today if they seriously thought there was no difference between defensible and indefensible views. Philosophy in the post-Enlightenment period (since the late eighteenth century) has become a most rigorous and demanding discipline, whose practitioners are more often lampooned for their intense commitment to precision and exactitude in the smallest details than for any presumed indifference to questions of right and wrong, either in the moral and social or in epistemic fields. It is precisely within the Enlightenment tradition that questions of right and wrong begin to be treated as needing the same agnostic discipline and openness of mind that has delivered progress in the natural and some social sciences. The proper intensity and discipline we expect in the pursuit of right and wrong is formulated and crystallised in the Enlightenment tradition, not abandoned in it. This is no proof against error, of course; but it is still as demanding a practice as there is. Where modern philosophers align themselves either seemingly or really with views annoying to SCAA, it is typically because their commitment to discerning right from wrong goes deeper than a lay audience's. Those who proclaim a similar commitment should pay greater attention to philosophy, not sweep it impatiently aside. From a philosophical point of view, the anti-intellectualism evinced here is no better – almost none other – than that of the relativism it offers to supplant.

For it is a travesty to represent modern philosophy as the triumph of relativism. First, there are plenty of modern philosophers who don't at all respect all beliefs and lifestyles – the existentialist, Marxist and postmodernist traditions are quite wonderfully intransigent, if that's what SCAA is looking for. (Nietzsche would not have tolerated the 'consensus' itself for a moment.) More seriously, where philosophers have sought to ground and justify tolerance, importantly for instance in the work of John Stuart Mill or of John Rawls today, it has never been a matter of facile moral agnosticism and has typically been an attempt to mould or to ratify the moral common sense of a liberal society; often in defence against precisely the kinds of authoritarianism (other than its own) which would horrify SCAA. Mill himself saw tolerance of diversity as enhancing the very pursuit of truth which the Report claims to be its own commitment. On top of this, there have been many serious attempts to revive ethical naturalism, a view of the moral as unequivocally this-worldly yet emphatically not 'relative'; and if communitarian views embrace a pluralistic world, they undermine the plausibility of a relativist choice for any individual.

Most pertinently, where education is concerned, Western philosophy has given birth to several traditions in the philosophy of education in which questions about values are not merely acknowledged but absolutely fundamental to most of what's written on education – the British analytic school of Hirst and Peters, the American pragmatist school derived from Dewey and the Frankfurt-inspired Critical Theory of education, amongst others. The possibility of rational discussion of values is actually fundamental to these traditions.

Of course relativist views are often also represented in modern philosophy, in the spheres of both the sciences and ethics. But even where this is so, relativism has rarely been propounded as a defence of moral indifference or vapid tolerance of what most of us find intolerable, whatever grounds we may or may not have for our views. Nor, in the scientific field, is it usually an attack on science; rather, it is usually an attempt to understand it. In both fields, when relativist views are advanced it is typically as an attempt, successful or not, to solve philosophical problems – which is to say, to make sense of the world and our knowledge of it.

Some of these problems of understanding do indeed stem from the success of science – a success which conservative spiritualists sometimes fear. It is difficult giving an account of the field of values in a culture whose most successful intellectual enterprise is the sciences. Accounts of values and of science must at least be compatible if they are both to be credible. But this is not, as one feels some 'spiritualists' view it, a craven capitulation to grubby materialism. On the contrary, it is grounded in the insight of eighteenth-century thinkers that if we are to take our culture seriously, then we must at least preserve our greatest intellectual success: and that is the rise of the sciences. Modern philosophical problems with value theory are not an abrogation of objectivity and rigour; on the contrary, they stem directly from the pursuit of objectivity and rigour.

However, the most interesting modern philosophical views are those forms of 'post-foundationalism' which, whilst denying the existence of 'foundations of knowledge' – basic truths on which all knowledge is built – nonetheless do not deny the differences between true and false or right and wrong, but rather describe them in quite different ways from the language of absolutes and essences. Views such as these (one might mention those of Rorty, Lyotard, the poststructuralists, modern philosophy of science and mathematics amongst much else) are often stigmatised misleadingly as relativist. This is a serious misunderstanding. Rather, they emphasise the importance of disciplined and open argument or of shared moral commitment in the construction of justice and knowledge, as a necessary replacement for the search for foundations. Open and disciplined argument may hope to contribute to an incomplete but improving understanding of right and wrong, true and false; a search for foundations or 'absolutes' cannot even do this much.

Postfoundationalist views require from the scandalised lay reader a greater effort of intellectual insight rather than an unreflecting recourse to antique assumptions. For instance, when the Report starts discussing 'core [moral] values', it writes that 'The question of absolutes [is] central to this debate.' Yet to say this is to presume against a welter of the best recent philosophy; and this cannot be justified by uncomprehending dismay at its results. One implication of much recent philosophy is that we have to take more responsibility for our views of right and wrong and give up the naive hope that a perception of 'absolutes' will solve our moral problems for us. Anti-relativists understand that 'truth' is one thing and 'what we agree on' is another; yet some, like the author of the Report, think we can disregard this problem once we start to talk about 'absolutes'. But to substitute, for instance, a conformist national agreement on values for a serious debate is precisely to indulge a relativist irrationalism rather than to identify right and wrong, notwithstanding the most hectic rhetoric of 'absolutes'.

Let it also be said that it is just illiterate to attribute philosophical relativism to a decline in religious belief. In the rigorous canons of philosophy, the existence of God has usually (not always) been thought neither here nor there in determining moral or epistemic issues. And this is not new. The philosophical schism between religion and the realm of 'moral absolutes' goes back as far as Plato in his dialogue the *Euthyphro*. (In the dialogue, Socrates asks Euthyphro whether piety is good because the Gods approve of it, or whether they approve of it because it is good. His aim is to detach questions of morality from questions of theology.) It is quite remarkable that the Report's author would appear never to have confronted this ancient and problematic debate. Does this reflect philosophical naivety in the culture of the SCAA 200? Or a manipulation of their views in this Report?

So, should we all be doing philosophy when thinking about education? Are philosophical discipline and a more serious regard for our own philo-sophical traditions what we really need to reform education and morality? This is precisely the kind of approach that seems disastrous to SCAA and supposedly to the SCAA 200. Whilst the objective of the whole SCAA exercise was to search for some kind of consensus, to do philosophy is not to look for consensus, it might seem, but rather to argue, interminably, inconclusively and corrosively. 'There was concern [whose concern?] that prolonging the philosophical debate may already have hindered practical progress in schools' (p. 10). So philosophy, some seem to think, is precisely what needs to be marginalised in such an exercise. (No room for the doubt here that the criteria of practical progress might themselves need philosophical examination.)

To think this is to suppose that we live our ordinary everyday lives innocent of philosophical beliefs and only entertain philosophical beliefs at rare, difficult or maybe comical moments. But this, surely, is wrong. People are invariably creatures of their historical context. To be human in the late twentieth century is just not like being human in the sixteenth or the twelfth. And what distinguishes the people of any epoch from another are sets of expectations, attitudes and beliefs many of which have the kind of generality and fundamental importance that deserves the name 'philosophical'. It is not that we acquire these beliefs through philosophical reflection, but that they go deeper than simple perceptions of fact and require philosophical reflection if we wish to repudiate or modify them (as the Report unwittingly tries to do). They have to do with attitudes to such things as the nature of truth, the path to knowledge, the importance of freedom or of conscience and so on. For instance, we moderns don't believe in magic; we do believe in investigation. We believe in the rights of the individual; we don't believe in human sacrifice. Where in any kind of society there is any kind of truly sustainable consensus, at least some philosophical ideas are part of it and for us these are typically those we have inherited from the Enlightenment. To refuse them any influence in our discussions is not to strengthen consensus but, quite the contrary, to betray our culture and identity, the intellectual resources by which we live.

Of course, the radically panicky can point today to a whole range of philosophical critiques of modernity and its discontents: critiques which this writer understands and in many cases agrees with. The Enlightenment gets a bad press these days and not wholly without good reason. This notwithstanding, my contention is that SCAA cannot possibly secure consensus precisely because it has repudiated too many of the philosophical assumptions and expectations which make us the modern people we are, and which even define for us what counts as a problem with modernity: its lapses of justice (particularly for marginalised groups), depredations of value (from the environment to the arts) and limitations in its realisation of rationality (in a rationalised economy). The same assumptions about justice, value or rationality and the expectations they prompt define what counts as an educational problem for us and a credible solution.

If the Report opts for grounding its view of moral education in spirituality, it does not recognise how dramatically it breaks from the Western cultural tradition of the past two hundred years in doing so. Whether its views are right or wrong, we should at least recognise how dramatic a rescension from the Enlightenment tradition they represent. For as we have seen, it is precisely from that tradition that we inherit our modern Western concern, to which these conferees appeal, for objectivity in the realm of knowledge, rational consensus in the realm of morals and the informing influence of both of these on the social structure of modern education no less than its actual content. My complaint is not that we cannot possibly criticise our Enlightenment heritage (as I have several times done myself, elsewhere), but that we should know what fundamental assumptions we address (one can bet the SCAA 200 are mostly horrified by postmodernism), see how much is at stake, and beware a lapse into the very relativism we wish to avoid if we repudiate our own guiding principles.

What then is the SCAA view of spirituality which so disregards our culture? Writing of the views expressed at the conference, the Report tells us that 'Spirituality was generally viewed as enriching individuals in their understanding of, and ability to relate to, others and of society as a whole' (*ibid.*, p.6). (And if SCAA is devoted to raising standards, could they please find a writer who can deal with English syntax?) But the eighteenth century Enlightenment, the fountain of Western secularism, was born, in part, of the view that spirituality actually impoverished our understanding, corrupted our human relationships, hindered material and educational progress and blinded us to the workings of society. We see examples of this still today – the social hermeticism of sects from the Moonies to Waco, the educational backwardness of the American Bible Belt, the spiritual zeal of the *fatwah* on Salman Rushdie, the (relativist) ineffectuality of New Age wackiness. It was not the view of Rousseau or the French *philosophes* or of Locke, Hume and Adam Smith, or of Tom Paine, Godwin or Shelley that the established churches had just got the wrong kind of spirituality and that meditation or metaphysical contemplation would turn the trick for a finer world. On the contrary, for them the world of the spirit was inherently one of darkness and 'superstition', by which they meant, at least in part, what we today would call 'neurosis'. It was 'the sleep of reason' which, for Goya, brought forth monsters. And well into the late nineteenth and early twentieth centuries, it was those artists, writers and even musicians least concerned for civility and the social (Symbolists, some abstractionists, *décadents*, Wagner, Bruckner, Nietzsche) who were pre-eminent amongst those who reached for the vocabulary of the spiritual. Rightly or wrongly, but certainly casually, the SCAA Report turns our culture on its head. It is much more radical than it seemingly intends to be.

This can be seen in the detail of the Report. The pages on 'Spiritual development' begin with a list of views apparently widely canvassed at the conference. And first, we are invited to agree that spirituality includes [*sic*] 'the essence of being human, involving the ability to surpass the boundaries of the physical and material'. Perhaps it would be unfair to quibble over the word 'essence' and to point out that it is encumbered with centuries of philosophical dispute. (Can one give a credible account of the essence of anything? Is the idea of an 'essence' perhaps empty or otiose? Does it carry useless ontological baggage? Commit us to untenable assumptions?) But one might have hoped that a report writer devoted to objectivity and (presumably) rigour might have avoided begging huge metaphysical questions and preferred the less tendentious phrase 'nature of being human'. Yet, of course, to use the word 'nature' is in itself to step away from the realm of the spiritual. If this is why the less presumptuous word was avoided, that in itself indicates what large assumptions are already being made without argument.

More pointedly, anyone with the slightest knowledge of their cultural heritage would surely remember those other canonic Western candidates for defining 'human nature'. SCAA may not have much use for a purely biological account; but it is hardly something to be swept to one side without argument. One would certainly have hoped the 200 would have remembered Aristotle's definition of man [*sic*] as 'a rational animal' and indeed as a *zoon politikon*; and would have hoped that educated people would know of the modern resurrection of this idea which defines human beings as the pre-eminent (perhaps only) language-using animals. Marx's notion of man as necessarily a labourer is hardly alien even to the liberal democratic tradition. (Margaret Thatcher seemed not to have much trouble with the idea). And the Enlightenment view of Man as the 'sovereign subject of knowledge' in a secular universe – Man the measure of all things – has informed higher education since the eighteenth century and, in the twentieth century, schooling too. And if it is this which is thought to have failed, this particular failure can hardly be laid at the door of trendy progressives. If this fails, so does most of our culture. In fact, let it be said that even the Christian view of human nature has not always put the spiritual at its centre. Part of the moral power of Christianity has always derived from its worldliness and the spiritual dimension of the Christian has often been defined only in her relation to God through prayer. Spiritual and mystical aspects of Christianity have often excited dissent within Christianity itself. The SCAA presumption as to the accepted 'essence of humanity' is a mightily impudent one.

Of course, a short report such as this is no place for elaborate arguments. But neither should it be a place for dogma or casual ignorance. One might reasonably ask for some recognition that the views expressed are by no means the small change of consensus nor by any stretch the taken-for-granted of our culture. If you want to stand up against your intellectual inheritance, the least you can do is to say so. This needs emphasising because most of the further reflections on spirituality are equally presumptuous.

These further reflections are rhetorically strung around two guiding contrasts: between 'inner' and 'outer' worlds and between this world and what transcends it, with all things bright and beautiful co-opted to the inner or the transcendent. So we are told (p. 6) that spirituality includes

- development of the inner life, insight and vision

so the insight and vision that really counts is that which derives from or is concerned with 'the inner life' – and presumably the insight of the creative scientist or vision of the progressive politician or artist is secondary if not unimportant;

- an inclination to believe in ideals and possibilities that transcend our experience of the world

so ideals which grow rather from our experience of the world – such as the certainty that people can behave better or live more fruitfully than they do – are lesser ideals; or else must be some unacknowledged glimpse of another world, unwitting testimony to the spiritual rather than intelligent responses to mundane existence;

- a response to God, the 'other' or the 'ultimate'

which without embarrassment defines spirituality as question-begging;

- a propensity to foster human attributes, such as love, faithfulness and goodness, that could not be classed as physical

so that whatever is not 'physical' must be spiritual – an empire builder's category mistake which assimilates all matters abstract to the spiritual – all emotions, ideas, customs, narratives, mathematical 'objects', scientific theories, social institutions – however intimately rooted in or connected to the physical, material, humanly biological and secular they may be; or as if a secular universe must be loveless, faithless and necessarily bad;

- the 'inner' world of creativity and imagination

as if works of art were not essentially public and as if their 'innerliness' trumps their public importance; as if they were not just as much material – in paint, sound, film, stage or printed word – as human beings, and as if that materiality were merely adventitious and secondary in each case rather than that of the public medium without which creativity is impossible.

I have indicated objections here, not because I take the alternative and secular view to be the superior (though in fact I do, in every case) but to indicate again the immense cultural presumption of this view of spirituality. I suggest that the alternative views are by no means unusual or eccentric within the modern world view, nor obviously amoral (far less immoral) or negligent of a concern for values. I also suggest that their consistent secularism relates them precisely to the high tradition of Western culture since the eighteenth century and to the concern for objectivity and defensible public norms which supposedly animates SCAA and its friends.

On the one hand, one of the fundamental themes of the development of western high culture has been precisely a struggle with, and often against, the ideas of the 'inner' and the 'transcendent'. And if these ideas are losing their grip on the best thinkers (often replaced by a new interest in the contrast between public and private), this is not for some lazy derogation of their calling but because the sternest critique of these ideas consistently shows them wanting. The idea of an inner world goes back to the medievals but takes its authority in modern culture perhaps primarily from the work of Descartes – he who formulated most compellingly the idea of a split between material and mental, 'outer' and 'inner'. Yet for a whole century now, this formulation has been under sustained attack in the tradition of philosophy, and the idea of the transcendent with it. Nor is this just a characteristic of empiricism or its latter-day versions in logical positivism and behaviourism, which are too often glibly identified with 'modernism' and taken for the very badge of the shallowness of modernity. Post-metaphysical thinkers of the stature of Wittgenstein, Heidegger, Ryle, Austin and Strawson, Gadamer, Adorno, Benjamin, Rorty or Quine, Habermas or Foucault cannot by any stretch of imagination be assimilated to the dogmatic dustbowl empiricism which makes such an easy target for conservative 'spiritualists'. Yet to see the commanding importance of their thought is to lose interest in the antique categories of inner and outer and of this world versus some 'other'; even where, as with Wittgenstein and Heidegger, there remains a space for 'the spiritual'. (If true spirituality there may be, it seems something unknown to the SCAA 200.)

On the other hand, none of this is to deny that Western culture also includes much profound exploration of the spiritual. It is not even to deny the validity of the category of the spiritual. Those who want a serious defence of spirituality can turn to the demanding work not just of Wittgenstein and Heidegger but of Kierkegaard, Buber, Bonhoeffer, Péguy or Eliot, and a wide range of music, poetry and painting. But to do so is immediately to abandon the world of consensus for that of the idiosyncratic, the searching and often the troubled and by the same token to concede the obligation to take the most sophisticated forms of secularism equally seriously. It is also to undertake a far more sophisticated account of the spiritual than could possibly fit the purposes of SCAA and its friends.

'But this is absurd,' cry the teacher, the administrator, the journalist, the parent. 'We can't be expected to take this stuff on board. It's far too deep, far too complex, far too alien – and why should we take your word for it that it matters?' But herein lies the rub: if you are not going to take more seriously the most advanced developments of your culture, then your claim to be concerned with defending standards, beating back relativism, standing up for objectivity and all the rest of it stands revealed as bogus. None of these values are defended by the parroting of received wisdom. They are sustained by traditions of disciplined enquiry, which of their very nature as often as not lead where received wisdom is most loath to follow.

In fact, one could say that this is a defining characteristic both of Western culture and of Western civilisation. In the scientific sphere we take it for granted. Scientists tell us strange and unlikely things – you might almost say, 'That's their job.' And what's more, so far from dismissing them as élitist cranks, we ground our technology on their results and theories and thus too our way and our standard of life. And we institutionalise the independence of scientists. Yet when it comes to philosophical issues and questions of right and wrong in education, we assume that we can assert 'basics' regardless of disciplined critique, and yet insist that in doing so, we defend objective standards. Absurdly, we defend morality from the attentions of disciplined enquiry. And this is intolerable – ethically, morally intolerable.

The way round these insuperable problems is to give up entirely the attempt to ground moral education in spiritual education. And is this really any loss? I mentioned earlier some contemporary manifestations of spirituality that any reasonable person must surely deplore. 'Oh indeed,' you can hear SCAA reply, 'you must, and we do, distinguish good from bad spirituality.' But any such answer would beg the question 'How?' And if one looks back at the claims made in the SCAA document, it seems clear that the covert criteria in use are ethical criteria – they speak of spirituality 'enriching individuals in their understanding of, and ability to relate to, others and of society as a whole' (p. 6). It seems that it is not grounding the moral in the spiritual but judging the spiritual by the ethical. And this is no surprise to philosophers. Since Kant and until very recently, moral philosophy has been guided by a belief in the autonomy of ethics – the view that moral considerations are the final court of appeal, whether or not they are conceived as 'absolutes', as independent of religion and 'spirituality' as of society and its politics. And this is not a derogation of moral rigour but its very instance.

'But still, something is missing' – surely this is where we came in with our painful reflections on Philip Lawrence and James Bulger. One can indeed agree that something is missing, but not spirituality. It looks very much as though spirituality is a stand-in, doing duty here for ethics – considerations on the question of 'the good life'. The issue of morality, of right and wrong, is obviously an aspect of ethics. But questions as to how to live well – to devote yourself to helping others or to the life of the mind, conformism or independence, religious or secular life, political engagement or aesthetic detachment, activism or stoicism? – questions such as these refer us to broader considerations than those of morality alone. Not all ethical values are strictly moral values concerned with right or duty.

As a society, we don't seem to take these broader questions seriously any more (though philosophers do). Yet without doing so, we will lack a sense of why life is worth living. And without that, morality is likely to seem an empty code. Youngsters need precisely such a sense of the value of life. (The Report recognises this, but lapses back into spiritual waffle.) But why then do ethical questions seem just naïve these days?

An ethical commitment to a particular kind of life presupposes the possibility of choice. But the choice involved is much more than consumer choice, or even 'lifestyle choice'. Living according to a reflective conception of what a life should be presupposes the possibility of an autonomous exercise of power, preferably in an open society. (Is spirituality what you have to make do with when you have no power and can't genuinely choose?) But education cannot provide this kind of power. It cannot even stimulate a yearning for it unless it is already a live social possibility. Rather, the possibility of serious ethical choice requires profound social reform; a serious address to what limits our possibilities in modern or post-modern society. An appeal to spirituality cannot provide this. It requires serious social, political and economic analysis. It also requires attention to our cultural heritage – an attention the SCAA 200 seem unprepared to give. (Besides, the exercise of autonomy is often seen as a threat to morality in contemporary conservative writing on education, if not in this document.)

It would be a relief to be able to conclude that when the Report talks about 'spirituality' and 'spiritual and moral development', it really means to say 'ethics' but has simply stumbled on the wrong word; and that my whole diatribe is a just fuss about nothing. This does not look plausible in the light of the claims about spirituality already examined. Nonetheless, there are other claims in the Report which beggar belief if we assume that 'spiritual' refers to the 'inner' and the 'transcendent':

Another possible channel for *spiritual* and moral development is citizenship education [p. 16, my italics]

Science teachers have a role in providing an objective, balanced and unsentimental approach to *spiritual* and moral issues [p. 13, my italics]

The conference agreed that *schools* are well placed to contribute to pupils' *spiritual* and moral development [p. 11, my italics]

and most stunning of all,

There was fear that technological and economic advances have marginalised spiritual values ... The paramount values are [now] primarily selfish ... There was widespread agreement that such values could undermine the well-being of society *and its supporting economy.* [p. 9, my italics]

Thus the SCAA view of the restorative value of spirituality can be readily endorsed by the Institute of Directors. Perhaps they do just mean ethics after all.

But ethics is a branch of philosophy and compatible with the secular and with Enlightenment humanism, all dangerously repudiated in the Report whilst just as dangerously misunderstood. Even if ethics is what they really mean, one would still need to complain about the SCAA view of philosophy. And the foolish things said about spirituality are even more foolish if taken to be really about ethics.

On the other hand, the Report links the spiritual much more closely, if not rigidly, to the religious. 'Spirituality', on any interpretation, is a relation of an individual to 'something else', here typically equated with 'absolutes'. But does not ethics also deal with absolutes? Certainly it often claims to deal with the universal, the categorical and the 'fundamental' (fundamental values). But to equate these with 'absolutes' is to make such human commitments 'thing-like' and to give them thus a metaphysical twist which mystifies them. It also 'privatises' them, inviting us to think of them as aspects of life to which we each relate directly, personally and even solipsistically – but nonetheless supposedly each in the same way – rather than relating to them as members of society engaged in serious debate and honest disagreement with each other on these important matters. And that's an ethical loss. To privatise, even in this roundabout way, consideration of something essentially social, how we live with each other, is to court the very disasters which SCAA wants to put right and to avoid by recourse to a bogus consensus on absolutes.

Spirituality, as the Report acknowledges (p. 12), owes much to silence and the meditative. (The spiritual is surely the backdoor by which the subjectivism of the 1960s will creep back in. Om!!) Ethics, on the other hand, is a social and cultural discourse with the longest tradition in Western civilisation (from Socrates, Pericles, even Solon). It owes everything to conversation and community. It is not concerned with the 'inner', the 'transcendent' or the supra-rational, unlike the discourse of the SCAA Report. Thus an appeal to spirituality and 'absolutes' simply shoves the Western tradition of ethics to one side.

So even if it's ethics that they want, as well or instead of spirituality, the SCAA 200 hare off – or are ushered off – in the opposite direction. In truth, they can't say what they want, in part because their conference seems to have forsworn any effort of clarification. That would involve it in all that obstructive philosophy stuff. Besides, it's so much easier to present a consensus if the group, as a group, is not encouraged to thrash out its disagreements, for then the disagreements can be judiciously overlooked. And it's no excuse to protest that the areas of agreement are the proper focus of attention. The question is whether the agreements are real or illusory.

So let me end where the SCAA Report effectively begins. Writing of the conference in question and its delegates, it claims 'There was *broad acceptance* [my italics] of the description of spirituality in *Spiritual and Moral Development* – a discussion document...', and there follows the list of the vapid spiritual claims resisted above. Such a 'broad acceptance' of the culturally bizarre would surely constitute as dismal a reflection as one might fear to see of cultural illiteracy. Is this perhaps a misattribution? We can only hope and pray that this is not a genuine illiteracy of the English professional classes, whose received wisdom is supposedly to be the touchstone of moral reform in education. If it is, Heaven help us indeed.

Chapter 11

Conclusion

We began this book by referring to the work of SCAA on moral education, and a full account of its rationale is given by its officers in Chapter 1. The work of the Forum is a reflection of widely held broader convictions about moral education and its high profile is undoubtedly shaping the terms of the current debate. It is appropriate for it to be given this prominence, therefore, in this book. We return to the Forum's arguments and standpoints in this conclusion to re-contextualise the wider-ranging discussions of our other contributors. At the same time we are trying to maintain a balance between the topical importance of the work of the SCAA Forum and perennial concerns about moral education.

The starting point, both for the Forum and for Tate and Talbot in their chapter above, is that a pervasive climate of relativism has 'struck at the heart of schools' confidence in the teaching of values'. Typical of this climate has been the question '*whose* values are we to instil?' put in a rhetorical way as if to defy any attempts to answer it. We see this rhetorical stance as a kind of adolescent reaction to the loss of certainty – if we can't be sure of anything whatever can we do? Such an attitude stands in the way of thoughtful consideration of moral education, as Talbot and Tate imply; it does not help us to face up to the difficulty of our moral lives, especially in circumstances of cultural pluralism. At a time of social change clear thinking about these matters is needed, and this can only be fostered by critique of existing positions, including that of SCAA and of those who have elaborated on its viewpoint.

Teachers' confidence has indeed been sapped and we welcome initiatives to counteract this. But we would locate teachers' lack of confidence in wider aspects of social and educational change in recent years, ones easy enough to identify when we recall the point of writing this book. Teachers have been on the receiving end of blame for the much-publicised 'decline in moral standards'. Working in a disparaged public sector, and in demoralising conditions, they have become easy targets for criticism and virtual whipping-boys for some politicians and journalists. We agree wholeheartedly that teachers need to have their confidence repaired. We doubt very much, however, that solutions to this are to be found in inservice training for teachers in the delivery of 'values education' any more than in improved mission statements for schools.

The National Forum for Values in Education and the Community was in part a response to concern that while much time and energy was spent on the promotion of pupils' academic development, their 'spiritual, moral, social and cultural development was being neglected'. But if their academic development was neglecting all this, it might be asked, what was it achieving? Unless, that is, the academic has become so diminished, so robbed of value ... and there are worrying signs that it has. What kind of academic development is it that does not touch all these areas? There is something odd about the idea of education without values – hence something odd about campaigns for values in education. The neglect of the types of development mentioned threatens not simply to reduce the worth of education but to deny it the title of education, properly so-called, at all. How could the academic not be a part of the cultural? How could the study of an academic subject not reflect on and be a part of our shared social world? How could it be pursued without some conception, however tacit, of the good?

But it would be misleading to say simply that 'values' have been neglected. The problem is rather that the wrong values have been promoted. The truth about the neglect of the spiritual, moral, social and cultural is that the dominance of a climate of instrumentalism has meant that a thin and impoverished conception of human lives has governed education. This does have effects in terms of the allocation of curriculum time but to see it in these terms is really to miss the point. Rather our very ideas of education and of knowledge and of human work have been debilitated, reduced to the 'essentials' (back to the 'basics') of supposed core and transferable skills. Once this reduction and fragmentation has taken place it is a mistake to imagine the damage can be undone by adding social education here, moral education there, and, not to forget, spiritual education over there. Our concern is not to advocate extended curriculum time for Personal and Social Education or for Moral Education.

The illusion that moral education might properly take place in this way is fostered by a partially distorted conception of the moral life – as consisting of issues and choices. This is something the Forum itself does not entirely escape. The prominence given to circumstances where people are faced with dilemmas, and especially with discrete and debatable dilemmas (abortion, blood sports, euthanasia), is apt to give the impression that morality is reserved for special occasions. Compartmentalising morality in this way has the effect of neutralising it or making it into a kind of side-show in our lives – suitable material for a parlour game ('Scruples', perhaps) or for a TV phone-in. This is a travesty of the ways in which our lives are never without moral significance, as we and our contributors have repeatedly tried to show. It is also symptomatic of the running together of our excessive preoccupation with individualism and the identity imposed on us as consumers. We think of ourselves as people who express ourselves through choices. To oppose someone's choice then looks like an unwarranted suppression of their individuality and authenticity, of what is closest and most real to them. No wonder we then hear that we should not be judgemental, that everyone's entitled to their opinion! No wonder that anything goes. When SCAA hopes that pupils will be able to *choose their own value system*, moral choice takes a characteristic aesthetic turn, just as you choose a colour scheme for your home. But values, and especially moral values, are not like that. We do not *choose* to think this is right and that is wrong. Normally we *cannot see things otherwise*: their rightness or wrongness forces itself on us. To change our values requires a more subtle and fundamental change of view. Moral education is then the last thing that could be 'bolted on'. Whether as good moral education or as bad, it pervades our schooling and our lives. Talk of 'values', even the title 'Forum for Values', plays into the hands of instinctive subjectivists (so often called 'relativists') since 'values' have the air of something personal to the individual.

The remit of the Forum was first to see if it could be 'demonstrated once and for all' that there are values upon which there is agreement across society. Very quickly the sub-groups charged with this task came up with a number of values that 'no-one of goodwill' could sincerely deny, irrespective of their race, ethnic group, religion, age, gender or class: these included friendship, justice, freedom, truth, self-respect and respect for the environment. Of course such values are like motherhood and apple pie – the first objection that Talbot and Tate consider – precisely because such values are part of our common humanity. But the very obviousness of these values, they say, especially where we have been preoccupied with respecting differences, may have made them invisible. Conclusive empirical evidence for the claim that these are values on which everyone of goodwill concurs is provided by the MORI poll which found that 95% of those consulted agreed.

Leaving aside the suggestion of circularity in 'everyone of goodwill', there seem here to be elements that may muddle future debate. There is a shift from empirical claims about whether or not people as a matter of fact hold certain values to the implication that these are somehow universal, and elsewhere that they are 'absolute'. If they are universal, why do not all the people consulted agree? The idea that these values are absolute, furthermore, is a metaphysical claim which could not be proved by any empirical research, let alone a MORI poll.

Paradoxically, the Forum sells morality and moral education short by appearing to rely on empirical evidence for claims that can only rest on ethical and philosophical argument. And this is odd because what above all the Forum ought to be doing, and in places clearly is doing, is making out the case for saying that morality is unavoidable: that it is an institution, manifested across a vast range of practices, without which we could not live a recognisably human life. What would it be like, after all, to live without weighing up the people around us and responding to them on the basis that they are, for example, trustworthy or liable to let us down, charitable or uncaring, truthful or deceitful? These are moral evaluations, and we make them constantly. It is hard to see how it could be otherwise. We are a moral, an ethical species. Unlike most of the animal world we have a degree of choice: we could decide to do other than we do. We are responsible for what we do in most respects but also in many respects for the way we are: natural hot-temperedness or impatience, for example, are qualities we should expect to be criticised for. But this truth about the human condition – that it is a moral one – does not warrant any claims that we share substantive values, except as a matter of contingent fact, or that such values are universal.

The search for agreement and consensus itself seems to cause confusion. For instance, *Education for Adult Life: the spiritual and moral development of young people* tells us:

> There were doubts as to whether there could be national agreement on core values. Employers, however, generally felt that there is little difficulty in establishing national core values. They pointed out that many organisations have developed statements of core values to which all employees can subscribe. Those engaged on school-based projects (for example, on citizenship education or readiness for employment) appeared to have no difficulty in producing lists of qualities desirable in young people. (SCAA, 1996, p. 10)

The confusion leads to another unfortunate shift: from national agreement on core values (presumably these are the kinds of values which no-one of goodwill would deny), to national core values (which presumably might not operate amongst other nations, whether inhabited by people of goodwill or not), to something like the organisational mission-statement, to lists drawn up by committees and working-parties. What are properly moral questions are not to be solved by people of goodwill making a list. The confusion is another inducement to lose sight of specifically *moral* values and moral argument.

Tate and Talbot are right to argue that productive disagreement depends on a level of agreement. Indeed the point could be put more strongly in that if there were no agreement about anything at all, we could not even communicate. But the problem with their notion of agreement here is that it is tied too much to the assumption that there must be clear-cut propositions on which we agree. Certainly people share reactions and responses at a quite basic, more or less physiological level – hunger, thirst, and much besides. What is less clear is that there must, therefore, be a set of values at a higher level they will all agree about. When Talbot and Tate say that there must be agreement on premises for there to be any argument, this is true in strictly logical terms. But what often lies behind an argument is precisely failure to agree on the premises, or failure to agree entirely what the terms used imply. Typically these are not differences that can be resolved by recourse to a dictionary; a whole perspective is taken for granted by one person, something different by another. 'We disagree so violently,' they argue in connection with the abortion debate, 'because each side believes that the other's acceptance of the premise – that human life, or human choice, ought to be respected – should entail the other's acceptance of the conclusion.' But is what perplexes us genuinely the failure of the other side to reason logically from these established premises? It may rather be that where other people do share these premises they do not interpret them in the same way. Their values – the substance they give to terms like 'respect for human life' – are different from ours. Where there are points of conflict, returning to the common ground does not always solve these – in fact, the common terms can mislead us as to what the common ground is.

In the absence of a belief in common values, is it true that 'anything goes'? It is not clear why this should follow. We can imagine a country in which individuals are loyal to one or the other of two communities in both of which values and behaviour are governed by a rigid code. Given that someone must be in one or the other community and that the communities do not have common values, how can it be the case for him or her that anything goes? Presumably the response must be that whatever values these communities apparently hold and whatever conflicts there appear to be, underneath there are values that they share and these are universal human values. But given the existence of situations not so different from the one described (Bosnia, for example) it is not clear how plausible this is, nor how far it gets us.

Acknowledging this, however, might cast the work of the Forum in a different light, making altogether more reasonable the exploration of values over which people can agree but radically altering part of the remit. It does seem reasonable to try to find out what values people in fact hold and then to see how this evidence can be used as a basis for guiding moral education in schools. It may be stimulating to share the views of those who are especially concerned with these matters – that is, the sort of people who make up the Forum. These might be seen as pragmatic measures to find a negotiated basis for policy. There is a gap, though, between this and the language of universals and absolutes. Agreement does not show which values are the right ones, even if it may provide a way for people to live peacefully together. The danger is in moving from a pragmatic approach to the assertion of metaphysical claims. And, we might note, the more such claims are absolutist in nature the more dissent and disagreement there is likely to be.

The Forum's concern is apparently not so much with difficult cases of moral conflict as with people who take the view that it is morally acceptable to beat up someone with whom one disagrees. Now it is doubtful whether someone who takes this view (or behaves as if they do) is really going to be open to *argument*. To put the emphasis on reasoned argument in such contexts is to lose sight of the kinds of lives that many people live and of the small part that is played by reasoned argument in relation to the density and variety of moral experience. This is not a comment only about thugs and muggers: the point is that the moral life extends for all of us into areas of our being where the views we explicitly articulate play but a tiny part. Failure to see this passes silently over the many ways in which dimly understood forces violently erupt into people's lives. Is *argument* necessary to convince us of what is right and wrong? More likely we pick up these notions at our mother's knee. As we grow up it is experience and experiences that make their mark on us, sometimes providing a sudden revelation, sometimes a slow dawning, of the wrongness of something which we hadn't before appreciated. Fiction can help us in this growing awareness, as Carole Cox's chapter shows. Explicit discussion also has its place – seriously discussing things with parents or friends or teachers, as Mary Midgley suggests. But even here it will be as much a matter of gradually coming to see what the terms of our premises amount to as of spotting a flaw in the reasoning. Serious discussion and reflection open the possibility of fresh descriptions: so much of the way we see things depends on the words we find to articulate them.

Still more to the point is the question of how one encounters the opinion that 'anything goes'. Typically this sentiment takes the form: 'Everyone's entitled to their own opinion. You shouldn't be judgemental.' It is worth remembering that sentiments such as 'anything goes' are seldom uttered by muggers and their like: probably they occur more in 'debates' about morality, where language can become dislocated and artificial, than in the real circumstances of people's daily moral experience. Most people who utter these words normally behave with no lack of conviction about what they and others should do concerning a vast range of moral matters. What often seems to be at issue here is less the much-discussed matter of *relativism* than what might be called 'moral feebleness': the reaction of the person who sees the mugging or the bullying and for whom 'Well, what can you do? You never know the background' (or similar) is a form of evasion, a refusal to be involved.

If argument is of relatively minor importance in moral education, how do we learn that mugging or rape are wrong? What kind of moral education has the mugger or the rapist received or failed to receive? Could we *tell* *them* what they need to know? No-one normally *teaches* their children that murder is wrong. To do so would be highly unnatural. It is interesting to consider how any of us learned that murder was wrong (as opposed, say, to learning that killing 'Red Indians' counted as murder). Probably we cannot remember because it is rather something we absorb as we grow up. The person who has not learned this does not need to be *told* about it: if they really cannot see it then it is unlikely that any explanation will cut much ice. What they need is a complete change of perspective. The apparent rehabilitative success in Canada and New Zealand of punishments that confront criminals with their victims appears to show how this can be brought about. Their whole picture of things shifts and then perhaps the horror of rape or the mean brutality of mugging dawns.

We have moved beyond questions of schooling but it is quite rightly a part of the Forum's remit to recommend how society in general might best help schools in the important work of moral education. Talbot and Tate see the Forum's statement of values as a tool that schools can use to elicit the help of society. We are of course all for the idea of helping schools and we agree that they often have an uphill struggle. We want to underline the extent and the causes of that struggle because we believe this is essential if good moral education is to become a reality.

Thus we must ask what exactly is meant by society, especially in view of recent pronouncements, such as Margaret Thatcher's, that there is no such thing as society, that there are only individuals and families. This opens a gap between the inward-looking unit of the family and the home and the impersonal forces of the state. Between the individual and 'our common humanity' the idea of *community* becomes eclipsed, as several of our chapters have tried to show. There is a weakness here which is written into many contemporary complaints about relativism. It is assumed that relativism must take the form of 'anything goes' and that, if the notion of universal human values is rejected, relativism is the only alternative. But in the making of this assumption, and however sensitive the subsequent working out of a statement of values, the truth of our embeddedness in community is passed over. The significance of the full title of 'The

National Forum for Values in Education and the Community', it is to be hoped, will not be forgotten. It is easy to think of community as something homogeneous and settled, as in the country with two mutually exclusive groups imagined above. But this is not true to our ordinary experience. Communities are fluid and changing and always inter-related with others, and often it is their tensions, internal and external, that give them their vibrancy.

Lastly, against the benefits of moral agreement and consensus the worth of a competing claim needs constantly to be evaluated: that it is a better prospect for humankind to live in a world where there are irreconcilable conceptions of the good and where values are seen and acknowledged to be disparate. Some would say that the challenge we are then presented with has the potential to lead us beyond the dangers of complacency and of hubris that have so commonly, not least in the twentieth century, been the failing of the human race. Perhaps in the moral life we have continually to acknowledge and respect real difference while seeking such agreement and consensus as we can find. A large part of moral education consists in learning how to achieve that fine balance.

Suggestions for further reading

This book has attempted to open different perspectives on moral education, drawing on strands of philosophy that are often neglected in discussions of moral education. Some of these ideas can be explored further by way of the reading that we list below.

Much debate about moral education and much of the philosophical literature on morality tends to be focused either on specific moral issues or on questions of moral principle. In this book we have steered in a different direction, however, because we believe that morality is a broader and less tidy matter than more familiar discussions tend to imply. A good short book that gives some sense of this is Iris Murdoch's *The Sovereignty of Good* (1970). In the three essays that make up this book Murdoch emphasises the importance of attention to particulars in the light of a vision of human nature that is at odds with prevailing assumptions.

Two accessible books on morality and ethics in general are J.L.Mackie's *Ethics: Inventing Right and Wrong* (1977) and Bernard Williams's *Ethics and the Limits of Philosophy* (1985). Alasdair MacIntyre's *A Short History of Ethics* has been regarded as a classic introduction for thirty years and has recently been reprinted (1997).

Several of the chapters in the present volume have emphasised the value of literature in understanding the moral life. The work of Martha Nussbaum provides a deeper exploration of some of the themes we raise. *The Fragility of Goodness* (1986) deals with Greek philosophy and literature while *Love's Knowledge* (1990) is focused more on more modern fiction, especially Charles Dickens and Henry James.

As for books that are more directly concerned with education, R. S. Peters's *Ethics and Education* (1966) was a standard text for many years. Graham Haydon's *Teaching about Values: a new approach* (1997) provides a helpful account of the central problems. Patricia White's *Civic Virtues and Public Schooling: Educating Citizens for a Democratic Society* (1996), is valuable in that it sets the political context for moral education. It is also worth reading some of the writings of John Dewey. Dewey's work is complex and rich, and should not be seen simply in connection with 'child-centred' education and the controversies that have surrounded it recently. *The School and Society* (various editions), for example, shows Dewey to have a deeper understanding of education and of its ethical nature than is often imagined. Readers interested in a text that tries to make sense of postmodern perspectives on education and which continually connects with matters of significance for moral education may be interested in our own *Thinking Again: Education after Postmodernism*, co-authored with Nigel Blake and Paul Smeyers (in press).

Carol Gilligan's *In a Different Voice: psychological theory and women's development* (1982) remains an interesting and important response to the widely influential ideas of Lawrence Kohlberg. Like Nel Noddings's books *Caring: A Feminine Approach to Ethics and Moral Education* (1984) and *The Challenge to Care in Schools* (1992) it registers the impact of recent feminist thinking.

Those who are interested in recent debates on spiritual education might read *Spiritual, Moral, Social and Cultural Development: an OFSTED discussion paper*, which was published in February 1994. Critical discussions of the topic are found in David Carr (1995 and 1996a and b) and in Nigel Blake (1996). There is also a collection of essays edited by Ron Best (1996) on the topic.

The Journal of Philosophy of Education frequently includes articles on matters in, or connected with, moral education, as do the *Journal of Moral Education*, the American journal *Educational Theory* and the Australasian *Educational Philosophy and Theory*.

Notes on the contributors

Nigel Blake is a philosopher of education who works in the Institute of Educational Technology at the Open University. His principal interests are in the politics of knowledge, particularly in higher education, and the debates on modernism and postmodernism. Recently he has been writing on the relation between educational experts and popular educational demands, and on the project of spiritual education. He is Vice Chair of the Philosophy of Education Society of Great Britain and Reviews Editor of the *Journal of Philosophy of Education*. He is co-author, with Paul Smeyers, Richard Smith and Paul Standish, of *Thinking Again: Education after Postmodernism*.

Carole Cox teaches English and Theatre Studies at Regent College, Leicestershire. She is the author of a number of publications in the field of philosophy of education and has made a special study of of the significance of the literary theory of F. R. Leavis for education.

Mary Midgley is the author of a number of books and numerous articles on philosophical matters. Her most recent publications include *Utopias, Dolphins and Computers* (Routledge, 1996) and *The Ethical Primate* (Routledge, 1996). She has also written many newspaper articles on ethical matters.

Michael Rustin is Professor of Sociology at the University of East London, and a Visiting Professor at the Tavistock Clinic. His work related to the field of psychoanalysis includes *Narratives of Love and Loss: Studies in Modern Children's Fiction*, with Margaret Rustin, (Verso, 1987) and *The Good Society and the Inner World* (Verso, 1991). He is co-editor of *Soundings*.

Anthony Skillen was born in Australia and came to Oxford to take a B. Litt. He now teaches philosophy at the University of Kent, He has always strained at the institutional leash and has been dismayed by the incuriosity of the schooled mind at all levels. Some of this was articulated in his *Ruling Illusions*, and in more recent articles in the *Journal of Applied Philosophy*.

Richard Smith is Senior Lecturer in Education at the University of Durham, and was until recently Director of Combined Studies in Social Sciences there. He is editor of the *Journal of Philosophy of Education*. His current research interests include the theory of social science and environmental ethics. He is the author of *Freedom and Discipline* (Allen and Unwin, 1985).

Paul Standish teaches the philosophy of education at the University of Dundee. He is the author of numerous articles and a book – *Beyond the Self: Wittgenstein, Heidegger, and the limits of language* (Avebury, 1992). Forthcoming publications include *Remembering Europe: nations, culture, and higher education* (Berghahn Books, 1997), the result of an international project co-organised and co-edited with Francis Crawley and Paul Smeyers. He is Depute Editor of the *Scottish Educational Review*.

Nick Tate has been Chief Executive of the School Curriculum and Assessment Authority (SCAA) since October 1994. He was previously Assistant Chief Executive with SCAA. Before this he was Assistant to the School Examinations and Assessment Council and Professional Officer at the National Curriculum Council. He has worked in schools and colleges of education in England and Scotland, with examination boards and with the Open University. He is the author of many books and articles on history and education. He was appointed Chief Executive-designate of the new Qualifications and Curriculum Authority (QCA) in January 1997.

Marianne Talbot is a lecturer in philosophy at Brasenose College, Oxford, and is the SCAA consultant charged with taking forward the work of the National Forum for Values in Education and the Community. Her specialisms are philosophy of mind and moral philosophy.

John White is Professor of Philosophy of Education at the Institute of Education University of London. His interests are in the interrelationships among educational aims and applications to school curricula, especially in the areas of the arts, history, and personal and social education. He has written extensively on educational matters and is the author of six books, the most recent of which is *Education and the End of Work: a New Philosophy of Work and Learning* (1997). In addition he has written over a hundred academic papers and chapters in books. He is a Vice President the Philosophy of Education Society of Great Britain, a Fellow of the US Philosophy of Education Society, Overseas Member of the Russian Academy of Education, and a member of the editorial boards of several journals.

Bill Williamson is Professor of Continuing Education at the University of Durham. His research and publications have been in the fields of the sociology of education, comparative education and social history, and are now centred on the sociology of lifelong learning. Formerly he taught Sociology at Newcastle Polytechnic and the University of Durham. He has worked in universities in Germany, Turkey and Egypt. He is currently working on projects concerned with the role of higher education in regional social and economic developments.

Bibliography

Aristotle (trans. W. Ross, 1969) *Nicomachean Ethics*, London: Oxford University Press

Bauman, Z. (1993) *Postmodern Ethics*, Oxford: Blackwell

Bauman, Z. (1995) *Life in Fragments: Essays in Postmodern Morality*, Oxford: Blackwell

Benson, J. (1983) 'Who is the autonomous man?' *Philosophy* 58, 5-17

Best, R. (1996) *Education, Spirituality and the Whole Child*, London: Cassell

Bettelheim, B. (1970) *The Informed Heart*, London: Free Press

Blake, N. P. (1996) 'Against spiritual education', *Oxford Review of Education*, 22, 443-456

Blake, N. P., Smeyers, P., Smith, R., and Standish, P. (in press) *Thinking Again: Education after Postmodernism*, Westport, Conn: Bergin and Garvey

Carr, D. (1995) 'Towards a distinctive conception of spiritual education', *Oxford Review of Education*, 21, 83-98

Carr, D. (1996a) 'Songs of immanence and transcendence: a rejoinder to Blake', *Oxford Review of Education*, 22, 457-463

Carr, D. (1996b) 'Rival conceptions of spiritual education', *Journal of Philosophy of Education*, 30, 159-178

Colley, L. (1992) *Britons: Forging the Nation 1707-1837*, New Haven and London: Yale University Press

Collier, G. (1997) 'Learning moral commitment in Higher Education', *Journal of Moral Education* 26.1, 73-82

Damasio, A. R. (1994) *Descartes' Error: Emotion, Reason and the Human Brain*, London: Macmillan

Freud, S. (1909) *Two Case Histories* ('Little Hans' and the 'Rat Man'), London: Standard Edition, Vol. 10

Freud, S. (1923) *The Ego and the Id*, London: Standard Edition, Vol. 19

Freud, S. (1929) *Civilisation and its Discontents*, London: Standard Edition, Vol. 21

Foot, P. (1978) *Virtues and Vices*, Berkeley: University of California Press

Gilligan, C. (1993) *In a Different Voice: Psychological Theory and Women's Development*, Cambridge, Mass.: Harvard University Press

Gilmour, I. (1992) *Dancing with Dogma: Britain under Thatcherism*, London: Pocket Books

Greenberg, J. and Mitchell, S. (1983) *Object relations in psychoanalytic theory*, London: Harvard University Press

Havel, V. (1991) *Letters to Olga*, London: Faber

Haydon, G. (1997) *Teaching about Values: a new approach*, London: Cassell

Hinshelwood, R. (1989) *A Dictionary of Kleinian Thought*, London: Free Association Books

Hutton, W. (1997) *The State To Come*, London: Vintage

Ignatieff, M. (1984) *The Needs of Strangers*, London: Chatto and Windus

Klein, M. (1986) *The Selected Melanie Klein*, ed. J. Mitchell, Harmondsworth: Penguin

Kohlberg, L. (1984) *The Psychology of Moral Development*, San Francisco: Harper and Row

Kraemer, S. and Roberts J. (1996) *The Politics of Attachment*, London: Free Association Books

Lovibond, S. (1983) *Reason and Imagination in Ethics*, Minneapolis: University of Minnesota Press

MacIntyre, A. (1981) *After Virtue: A Study in Moral Theory*, London: Duckworth

MacIntyre, A. (1997) *A Short History of Ethics*, London: Routledge

Mackie, J. L. (1977) *Ethics: Inventing Right and Wrong*, Harmondsworth: Penguin

Meltzer, D. (1973) 'Terror, Persecution and Dread,' in: *Sexual States of Mind*, Perthshire: Clunie

Moore, W. (1953) 'Lot', in Aldiss, B. (ed.) 1961, *The Penguin Science Fiction Omnibus*, Harmondsworth: Penguin Books

Murdoch, I. (1970) *The Sovereignty of Good*, London: Routledge

Noddings, N. (1984) *Caring: A Feminine Approach to Ethics and Moral Education*, Berkeley, Cal.: University of California Press

Noddings, N. (1992) *The Challenge to Care in Schools*, Nw York: Teachers College Press

Nussbaum, M. (1986) *The Fragility of Goodness*, Cambridge: Cambridge University Press

Nussbaum, M. (1990) *Love's Knowledge*, Oxford: Oxford University Press

OFSTED (1994) 'Spiritual, Moral, Social and Cultural Development: an OFSTED discussion paper', February

Peters, R. S. (1966) *Ethics and Education*, London: Allen and Unwin

Phillips, M. (1996) *All Must Have Prizes*, London: Little, Brown and Company

Reynolds, D. (1995) 'The effective school: an inaugural lecture', *Evaluation and Research in Education*, 9:2, 57-73

Rieff, P. (1959) *Freud: The Mind of the Moralist*, London: Gollancz

Rosenfeld, H. (1987) *Impasse and Interpretation*, London: Tavistock

Rustin M. E. and M. J. (1985) 'The Relational Preconditions of Socialism', in: Richards, B. (ed.) *Capitalism and Infancy*, London: Free Association Books

Selznick, P. (1994) *The Moral Commonwealth: Social Theory and The Promise of Community*, Berkeley: University of California Press

Steiner, J. (1993) *Psychic Retreats*, London: Routledge

SCAA [School Curriculum and Assessment Authority] (1995, first published 1993) *Spiritual and Moral Development*, Discussion Paper No. 3, PO Box 590, London SE5 7EF

SCAA [School Curriculum and Assessment Authority] (1996) *Education for Adult Life: the spiritual and moral development of young people*, Discussion Paper No. 6, PO Box 590, London SE5 7EF

Taylor, C. (1995) 'A most peculiar institution', in: Altham, J. E. J. and Harrison, R. (eds.) *World, Mind and Ethics*, Cambridge: Cambridge University Press

Van Reid, R. (ed.) (1992) 'Reading the Future – A place for Literature in Public Libraries', seminar held in York, 3 March, 1992, 15-18

Warnock, G. (1971) *The Object of Morality*, London: Methuen

White, J (1990) *Education and the Good Life*, London: Kogan Page

White, J (1995) *Education and Personal Well-being in a Secular Universe*, London: Institute of Education

White, J (1997) *Education and the End of Work: a new philosophy of work and learning*, London: Cassell

White, P. A. (1996) *Civic Virtues and Public Schooling: Educating Citizens for a Democratic Society*, New York: Teachers College Press 1996

Williams, B. (1985) *Ethics and the Limits of Philosophy*, London: Fontana

Wilkinson, R. (1996) *Unhealthy Societies: The Afflictions of Inequality*, London: Routledge

Winnicott, D. W. (1965) 'Psychoanalysis and the Sense of Guilt', in: *The Maturational Process and the Facilitating Environment*, London: Hogarth Press

Wolfe, A. (1989) *Whose Keeper? Social Science and Moral Obligation*, Berkeley, Cal.: University of California Press

Wollheim, R. (1971) *Freud*, London: Fontana

Wollheim, R. (1993) 'Desire, Belief and Professor Grunbaum's Freud', in: *The Mind and its Depths*, London: Harvard University Press

Index